FORK*lore*

RECIPES AND TALES FROM AN AMERICAN BISTRO

ELLEN YIN

TEMPLE UNIVERSITY PRESS

PHILADELPHIA

Temple University Press
1601 North Broad Street
Philadelphia PA 19122
www.temple.edu/tempress

Published 2007

Printed in China

Text design by Paragraph, Inc.

Library of Congress Cataloging-in-Publication Data
Yin, Ellen.
    Forklore : recipes and tales from an American bistro / Ellen Yin.
        p. cm.
    Includes bibliographical references and index.
    ISBN-13: 978-1-59213-651-3 (cloth : alk. paper)
    ISBN-10: 1-59213-651-6 (cloth : alk. paper)
        1. Cookery, American. I. Title.
TX715.Y35 2007
641.5973—dc22   2007017370

2 4 6 8 9 7 5 3 1

contents

list of recipes

acknowledgements

Over the past ten years, many people have contributed to making this book possible and Fork a tremendous success, especially friends, family, staff, purveyors and customers. It is impossible to list everyone, so please forgive me if you've been a part of Fork and I haven't mentioned you by name.

To the chefs who have made this book possible and tolerated all of my changes, comments and expectations over the years: Thien Ngo, Anne-Marie Lasher and Dave Ballentine.

To the hundreds of staff who have believed in Fork and worked to raise the standard of Fork, particularly Monica Barry, Deborah Brandler, Dalila Butler, Robert Caporusso, Adam Carangi, Megin Cave, Ashley Cobbett, Juliet Conti, Lisa Crumrine, Tony DeMelas, Lauren Derstine, Karen Gibson, Wren Ingram, Susan Johnston, Rebecca Kimball, Brian Martin Scott, Christina McKeough, Michael O'Halloran, Paul Rodriguez, Rachel Rogala, Guy Smith, Vernon Sweet, Gigi Tevlin-Moffat, Wayles Wilson and Stephen Wood

To those artists who helped make Fork beautiful: Marguerite Rodgers, Drew Miller, A. J. Lewis Corporation, Kevin O'Brien, Dennis Haugh, Melani Lewandowski, Trevor Dixon, Pete Checchia and the staff at Paragraph, Inc.

To friends who have helped me along the way: Jerry Blavat, June Kinney, Anna Tasca Lanza and Max McCalman

To Clare Pelino, Micah Kleit and Janet Benton, who helped me have the confidence to put the book together over the past year

To Tara Mataraza Desmond, who interpreted my notes patiently and tested all of the recipes, and Lydia Navatsyk, who helped review and edit the text in its earliest stages

To my mother and my two brothers, Mark and Ken, who have supported my efforts regardless of direction, and to my father, who passed away before seeing Fork but whose love helped make me who I am today

To my inner circle of creativity, Wayne Aretz, Bob Aretz and Kevin Hills, who continuously help inspire, design and create so many great ideas

To my partners, Jay Kossman, Phil Kamp, Richard Radoccia, Ron Perrone, Monica Sella, Barbara Sella, Antonio Sella and especially Roberto Sella, whose friendship and support over the past fifteen years form the basis of so much of this book

Thank you to you all; Fork would not be the same without you . . .

introduction

**IN SEARCH OF
AMERICAN CUISINE**

WALK INTO ANY RESTAURANT—a diner, a bar or a fine dining establishment—and you'll find that it has its own unique culture. And the longer a restaurant is in business, the further ingrained that culture becomes. Of course Fork is no exception. After ten years, having worked with roughly six hundred employees and served well over a half million guests, we certainly have a story to tell.

From the beginning, our goal at Fork has been to serve simple, unpretentious, New American bistro-style cuisine in a casual but sophisticated environment. Because the industry is so competitive, a restaurant that doesn't reinvent itself on an ongoing basis doesn't survive. Fork has been flexible enough to survive shifts in eating trends, new competition, the growth of Philadelphia and fluctuations in the economy because we are constantly asking ourselves the question, "What is a New American bistro?" All of our answers have started with being open to new ideas. From the beginning, Fork has been fluid. If something didn't work, we'd adjust it, fix it or tweak it to make it work.

However, it would be false to imply that this fluidity alone explains our success. The formula for a successful restaurant is almost impossible to nail down. Is it the location, the food, the service, the interior? Good food is obviously important, but as our current chef Thien Ngo says, "If you are hungry enough, the food will

1

Ellen, mom and auntie

taste good!" To keep a restaurant going for ten years as we have, you need more than just good food. You also need more than a good location, good service and a beautiful interior. To succeed over the long haul, a restaurant has to have a clear, concise and consistent vision. While we have worked incredibly hard to do everything well, we have worked just as hard to make all of our efforts support our vision of a simple, elegant bistro that serves delicious, reasonably priced food and provides friendly service that makes you want to come back soon.

CHINESE JERSEY GIRL

People are always curious to learn how chefs or owners enter the restaurant business. Although a lucky few know their career calling right away, the rest of us figure it out by trial and error. Of course, we all have one thing in common: a love of good food.

During my childhood, good food was a part of my daily life, thanks to my mother, Ching Yun Yin. Although many of our relatives and friends took her good cooking for granted, my brothers and I had a sense that our nightly dinners were a cut above normal home cooking. Whereas other kids our age were eating meatloaf, pot roast, pasta or chicken, we were treated to a smorgasbord of five or six different traditional Chinese dishes every night; seaweed, jellyfish, braised oxtails, chicken feet, roasted duck in soy sauce, prawns with their heads on and steamed whole fish were among the usual dishes at the table. Because my mom's family was originally from Shanghai and my father's family was from Hunan, she exposed us to a variety of ingredients and made specialties from different regions of China.

Some of my fondest childhood memories include sitting at the kitchen table with my grandmother and my mom, rolling and wrapping dumplings. I would listen to my mom and grandmother describing how to make the perfect dumpling, elaborating on its consistency, size, filling and cooking method. Then, when I was in high school, I started baking simple fruit breads, brownies and cakes in my home economics class. Soon, I was experimenting with all kinds of baking recipes. I couldn't wait until I was old enough to get a job in a restaurant kitchen so I could learn more about cooking.

The summer I turned sixteen, I began working at the Chinese Kitchen, a small restaurant just outside our town of Rumson, New Jersey. It was a tiny place that specialized in Mongolian barbecue. Even though Rumson was a bedroom community for New York, the Chinese Kitchen was considered exotic at the time. Raw meat would be sliced to order, marinated in a sauce customized by each guest and cooked on a special Mongolian barbecue grill. The owners had another restaurant as well, and since the menu at the Chinese Kitchen was so limited, I wanted to work at their other location as soon as I had mastered that job. At the second

Ellen Yin

restaurant, I helped make spring rolls, fried rice and other simple foods. The kitchen was located by the entrance to the dining room, and I enjoyed catching glimpses of people enjoying their meals, or overhearing the conversations of the waiters and waitresses. Everything about that restaurant fascinated me.

I started out in the kitchen, but the more I worked, the more intrigued I became by the idea of serving people. So I applied for a job as a busser at the

Fromagerie, the most upscale restaurant in the area, which was just around the corner from where we lived. It had an excellent reputation throughout New Jersey and was one of the few restaurants in the area that had been reviewed by the *New York Times*. In the early 1980's, people still considered French food the epitome of gourmet cuisine. I remember how I felt when I pushed open the restaurant's heavy wooden door for the first time. The door reminded me of the entrance to a mansion, and when I entered the restaurant and looked around, I suddenly became very nervous. I had never eaten at a restaurant that had tables set with fine tablecloths, multiple pieces of silver, fancy china and stemware. At home, we just used chopsticks and maybe a spoon.

Sidewalk café

Despite my anxiety, I applied for a job there, and I was hired as a busser. For the next two years, the Fromagerie was my hobby. I became friends with the other bussers, servers, cooks and bartenders. And working there exposed me to foods I had never tasted before, such as fettuccine Alfredo and quiche. My mom never cooked with cream or butter, and we certainly didn't eat cheese at home. The blue varieties struck me as particularly stinky and unappealing at first. I can't say that I became a total convert, but at least I would try cheese on occasion. I also learned a lot about desserts, because the Fromagerie made its own pastries. At home, I tried to replicate pastry recipes from the restaurant and tested them out on my family—until my father finally said, "No more desserts, unless you help us eat what you make."

That year, when I was eighteen years old, I declared my goal to open a restaurant after college. But my parents thought that I would have more financial security and an easier career if I became a doctor or an engineer. As a compromise, I entered the University of Pennsylvania's Wharton School in Philadelphia to study economics and business. Because Penn was only an hour and a half away, I would rush home on the weekends to visit my friends at what we called the Fromage. But eventually I realized that I didn't have to go home to be in a restaurant. I got a job at the Conversation Cafe, a dingy basement cafe in Penn's Student Activity Center. Business was slow, and when the owner asked if I had any ideas, I suggested serving

Fork 1997

desserts in addition to pastries. The next thing I knew, I was making them in my dorm room in a toaster oven.

Yet even my efforts could not save the cafe from closing. Next I found a job as a server at the only French restaurant near campus, La Terrasse. Immediately life seemed exciting again. La Terrasse served simple, traditional French cuisine with an Asian twist. That summer, I stayed in Philadelphia instead of going home. In less than a year, I had formed new restaurant friends (many of whom are still my closest friends) and met many customers, some of whom now come to Fork.

In my junior year, one of my classes required students to form teams to come up with plans for a new business. A bartender at La Terrasse named Wain Ballard and I put together a business plan for the Harmony Cafe. Interestingly enough, the proposed cafe was located in Old City at the corner of Third and Arch Streets, a block away from Fork. Although I learned a lot through this effort, the project gave me a glimpse of a harsh reality: my dreams needed capital to fuel them. Without any angel investors or my own money, I had to put my ambitions on hold and settle for looking for a "real" job after graduation.

Ellen and Roberto, 2001

Over the next five years, I held various jobs in advertising and fundraising, but I couldn't stay at any one for more than a year. However excited I was at the beginning of each job, I quickly became bored. At least I was narrowing down my options! Finally I decided to return to school to try once again to figure out "what to do with my life." Two years later, I graduated with an M.B.A. in health care administration from Wharton and began my job search again.

At that point, I had lived in Philadelphia for almost ten years, and the city had already begun to change for the better. It was even selected as one of the best U.S. cities in which to live. I had formed even more friendships by then and really didn't see how any out-of-town job could entice me to give that up. Also I was learning a lot about planning and developing a business at my new job at a health-care consulting firm. Yet even after I became an independent consultant, I continued to dream about opening a restaurant. I craved the creativity that had been missing in all of my other jobs. I loved food, entertaining and serving people, and I devoured any books or magazines I came across that were related to restaurants, food reviews or cooking.

I still remember the moment when I decided to try to make my dream a reality. I was thirty-one. While sitting in a bookstore, I picked up a copy of *Food & Wine* and realized that almost every featured restaurateur was between the ages of twenty-five and forty-five. If they could do it, why couldn't I? If I failed, I could always go back to the kind of work I was doing already.

But however determined I might have been to make a go of my dream at last, I knew I couldn't do it alone. So I began to talk with those closest to me about my plans. Many of my friends had listened patiently to my career complaints over the years, including Roberto Sella, a classmate from graduate school. Roberto's academic interest in finance was so different from my focus on health care that I was surprised our paths had crossed. Yet ever since I have known him, Roberto's passion has been wine. Over the years we had organized many dinner parties for groups of friends. Often, after enough wine, he and I would begin to discuss opening a restaurant and to choose the types of food and wine we would serve. So when I announced that I was ready to open a restaurant, Roberto couldn't wait to be a part of it. Roberto always loves a new project, and this one would gain him a decent place at which to drink his own wine!

With both of us eager to pursue a venture that incorporated our passions for food and wine, Roberto and I started on an exciting journey.

According to industry experts, location is the most important predictor of a restaurant's success. If a restaurant closes, its failure is often attributed to a bad location. But what really makes a good location?

Because I have an M.B.A., you might assume that I had a complex formula for determining the right location for my dream restaurant, perhaps one created during my graduate-school independent study, which assessed the feasibility of locating a Taco Bell in Center City Philadelphia. However, I had no such formula. My strategy for choosing a location for our restaurant was simple. It started with looking for a neighborhood where I really liked the architecture.

After riding my bike around Center City, I decided to focus on Old City, a historic district on the east side of town. The industrial lofts, the art galleries, the integration of old and new businesses appealed to me. And there was a vacant space on the 300 block of Market Street where the building owner wanted a restaurant. Our neighbors would be a dollar store (which later became the site of Fork:etc) and Pants Corner Plus, one of two men's clothing stores owned by feuding brothers (the other being Shirt Corner). Although they might not have been

306 Market Street, pre-Fork

the typical neighbors for an upscale restaurant, all three businesses represented the history of Market Street as a retail area. Their distinct signs, which are painted onto the buildings' facades, are noted in the City of Philadelphia Historical Commission records, and they serve us well as landmarks when we are directing guests to Fork. The two brothers became regular customers of the restaurant. Old City is also home to the Liberty Bell, Philadelphia's biggest tourist attraction at the time; to Franklin Court, once home to Benjamin Franklin; and to the legendary restaurant Old Original Bookbinder's. Old City had already been recognized as the gallery district, and home design and furniture stores were cropping up along Third Street, one of the primary retail blocks of the neighborhood and right around the corner from the available site.

The space itself was a major consideration. Standing in front of a building that looked like a construction site, I had a difficult time envisioning a restaurant there. But the inside impressed me, with its soaring, fourteen-foot ceilings and its cast-iron pillars bearing coat upon coat of paint. The scale of the room was grand, and its width was double that of an ordinary building on the block. In Philadelphia, land of the rowhouse, wide spaces are hard to find. Still, some people, including Roberto, were not impressed by the space or the location. For many years, the east side of Market Street had been underdeveloped, and this building was no exception. Built in 1896, it was a shell that needed a new physical and mechanical infrastructure and a new façade. In addition, a fire in the rear of the building had damaged the ceilings and floors.

Despite everyone's concerns, however, I thought the building was perfect. So I frantically started writing a business plan to justify the location and rent to the bank before someone else nabbed it. The more I analyzed the area, the more obvious it seemed that the neighborhood had the potential to blossom. The residential population of Old City was growing, and the demographics were right for the type of restaurant we wanted to create. The local businesses were stable, and our restaurant would be within

Enjoying a staff beer during an electrical outage, 2000

walking distance of some of Philadelphia's largest corporations. The arts
were also thriving: Old City is home to two performing-arts theaters,
three movie theaters and many new art galleries, and the neighborhood's
reputation as an artists' community draws people to special events such as
First Fridays, when galleries open their doors for evening receptions on
the first Friday of each month. The City of Philadelphia had just invested
thirty-one million dollars into the streetscape and intended Market Street
to become the pedestrian walkway from the new Convention Center to
the proposed waterfront development. And amid all of this possibility,
competition from other eating establishments seemed like it was going
to be minimal; in 1996, only a few upscale dining establishments existed
within a seven-block radius of the possible site of our restaurant.

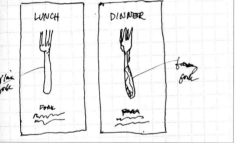

Bob's sketchpad from brainstorming session, 1997

Fortunately, by the time I had finished the business plan, Roberto was convinced of the feasibility of the location and the bank was, too. From the beginning, positive energy surrounded the project. Whatever the explanation—whether it was luck or good feng shui—things were going our way. (Feng shui is the Asian belief that the placement and positioning of objects in our surroundings affects both our energy and our level of success. The building's good feng shui was later confirmed by a local feng shui master!) And I was discovering a big part of the fun of opening a restaurant: everyone wants to be involved. Within my circle of friends, many were excited to help. Luckily for me, they were not only enthusiastic but talented as well! I attribute a large part of Fork's success to the many people who helped create it.

After choosing the location and obtaining financing, we hired Marguerite Rodgers, one of the city's most talented interior designers, to create the visual concept for the space. While the restaurant was being designed, a small group of us met on my living-room floor to brainstorm together about names and concepts. Around me sat some of my most creative friends—my boyfriend, Wayne Aretz; his brother, Bob, who owns Paragraph, Inc., a brand agency; Dennis Haugh, a trompe l'oeil artist who painted the faux finishes and lampshades that soon became a signature of Fork's interior; Paul Rhodes, my roommate of four years who knew the restaurant business inside and out; and Mark Tasker, a pastry chef at the famous Balthazar Restaurant in New York.

In my thoughts before we met that day, one idea stood out: I wanted a restaurant sign that bore an icon rather than words. During my travels as a consultant, I had come across a hip bar in Soho called Match whose sign was a single matchbox. I loved its simplicity and sophistication. So I had that in mind while ideas were being thrown around in my living room, some of which played upon the historic nature of the street (which had been named High Street until 1853), the history of the building (which had held a dry goods store) and the address (306 Market Street). Then I glanced to my side and saw Bob Aretz's drawing pad, on which he had sketched a fork. "Fork. That's interesting," I thought. "But maybe it's too close to pork or, worse yet, the F word." I could hear the word in action, and not all of the associations were positive: "Fork you. Put a fork in it. Fork it over." Yet I was intrigued by the word and by the novelty of having such a short name. One-word, one-syllable restaurant names are the norm now, but in the late 1990's, they hadn't taken off yet in Philadelphia. I also liked the way "fork" sounded; it was simple, blunt and not easily forgotten.

When I spoke my thoughts to the group, Bob also got excited. And the more we brainstormed about "Fork," the more adamant he became about having no written words on the sign. The icon, he insisted, should be the restaurant's only identifier. He felt that this would give the restaurant a special quality, and he was right: to this day, seeing the simple fork on the door makes some people feel that they've stumbled on a real find. We also decided that day to make forks a part of our design theme. Forks even appear on the mosaic threshold at the entrance to the restaurant, which depicts a Roman table.

Since we knew that the interior of the restaurant would incorporate the old architecture into a contemporary design, we decided to echo this mixture of old and new in the decor. So we bought up as many silver-plated forks from local antique shops as we could. We planned to combine them with simple, modern knives and spoons. Even our first chef, Anne-Marie Lasher, and her father have helped in our ongoing quest for antique forks; she received a collection of silverware from her father, Doug Lasher, who was a former caterer, and she donated the forks to the restaurant. Doug, who lives in New Hampshire, continues to visit flea markets throughout New England in search of forks for us. But now I'm getting a little ahead of my story.

vision for food: early recipes

Although our plan sounded good in writing, Roberto and I knew that creating a great restaurant concept required finding a great chef. That meant months of networking, interviewing and auditioning chefs. We felt as though we were trying to find a needle in a haystack until serendipity stepped in. I ran into a former coworker from La Terrasse, whom I had not seen in ten years, and asked if he knew of any chefs we might want to consider. He handed me the phone number of Anne-Marie Lasher, a graduate of Bryn Mawr College who had become interested in food because her father had a catering business. After college, she decided to work in a restaurant kitchen, and she rose from line cook to kitchen manager in less than a year. Although we had never crossed paths before, Anne-Marie and I had both worked at the White Dog Cafe in West Philadelphia. I worked there for a year as a bartender, and she worked there for nine years and rose to the position of executive sous chef.

The White Dog was located right next door to La Terrasse, and owner Judy Wicks had spent her early years in the restaurant industry managing and running La Terrasse. From there, she helped create Urban Outfitters, a retail business that has become a national chain. Finally she opened the White Dog Cafe, following in the footsteps of Alice Waters of Chez Panisse in Berkeley. Whereas the local-foods movement had taken off by then on the West Coast, the White Dog was one of the only Philadelphia restaurants that made a special effort to use locally grown or organic ingredients and to support local agriculture. On top of that, Judy has always been a community-oriented person, forming relations with sister restaurants in third-world countries and promoting discussion of important issues related to government, economic development, race and more. She even provided funding and space for a foundation for sustainable agriculture within the cafe. A woman with an acute business

acumen and a true social-entrepreneurial spirit, Judy Wicks has provided
a training ground for a whole new type of Philadelphia restaurant.
Numerous restaurants and food businesses run by former La Terrasse
or White Dog employees have emerged over the past twenty years.

All of this meant that our connection through the White Dog Cafe
was meaningful to Anne-Marie and me. And the first time we met,
we clicked. So I was anxious to see if we had a consistent vision for the
menu. The business plan, which we had created prior to meeting Anne-
Marie, described our food concept as bistro style with French and Asian
influences, much like the cuisine of La Terrasse. Although Anne-Marie's
cooking style was clearly American, that didn't bother us because we
sensed that she would be a hard worker. During her audition, she made
three dishes for us. With such limited exposure to her cooking, it was
difficult to tell her real capabilities. Still, Roberto and I chose her to be
our first chef and partner, and the three of us began working together
to create a food vision.

Chef Anne-Marie Lasher

Over the next six months, the more we talked, the more defined our
vision became. The three of us agreed that the food should be simple,
unpretentious and moderately priced. We all wanted to use the best
ingredients so that they could speak for themselves, without having to
be masked by complex sauces. We agreed, too, that the menu would
change to keep diners interested and to follow the seasons. And Roberto
and I wanted Anne-Marie to cook what she did best. Naturally her style
reflected that of the White Dog, where she had spent most of her culinary
career. As we got to know each other better, we found that hers was an
eclectic style of cooking, distinctly American but influenced by many
ethnicities. We decided to call it New American bistro-style cuisine.

We had made a lot of progress, but we still had to come up with an
arsenal of actual dishes to serve when we opened. We needed a lot of
dishes because the menu would be changing so frequently. So in the
summer of 1997, Roberto's home became a test kitchen. Anne-Marie

would try out recipes, and we would invite various friends to give feedback about these potential menu items. That summer, Anne-Marie really blossomed as a chef. Her food was tasty, flavorful and fresh. We would argue over dinner about trivial things such as whether zucchini should count as a starch or a vegetable in an entrée, whether we should serve white zinfandel and which china and stemware we liked best. But for the most part we were all just really excited to open.

When we finally opened in October 1997, Fork was one of the first affordable, stylish restaurants to appear in Philadelphia in a while. Many people even credit Fork for pushing Old City into the fine dining arena. To me, we were just in the right place at the right time. But this wasn't necessarily evident at the start. As is true for any new restaurant, our first few weeks were shaky. Even so, to the credit of our opening staff, things went surprisingly smoothly. We needed more diners, though, so at the beginning Roberto and I were calling everyone we knew to get people to come. I was nervous about whether we could pay our bills and whether the waitstaff would make enough money to stick with us. Of course we knew that a newspaper review would help raise our visibility, and fortunately our first review appeared in the *Philadelphia Weekly* just a week after we opened. This review kick-started our business, so by November we were able to open for lunch and Sunday brunch. Only a month after we opened, weekends were booked and more reviewers began to appear. Then our publicist convinced a *USA Today* reporter to visit Fork, and in December the newspaper featured Fork as one of only four restaurants in Philadelphia to check out.

By this time, Anne-Marie's cooking style had really begun to develop. Menu items were evolving every few days, which also made us an unusual addition to the restaurant scene. At that time in Philadelphia, the concept of a truly evolving menu didn't exist. Chefs would change menus every quarter and add daily or weekly specials, but none had implemented menu changes beyond this. Thus Fork was unusual: we printed our menu anew almost every day.

First Course

Creamy Wild Mushroom- Corn Chowder · 3.50

Port- Roasted Pear
with Watercress, Endive and Stilton · 5.50

Salad Greens in White Balsamic Vinaigrette with
Homemade Mustard- Seed Bread Stick · 4.50

Grilled Coriander Shrimp over Spinach Salad with
Curried Yogurt Dressing and Almonds · 7.75

Herb Wood- Smoked Trout with Cucumber- Caper Relish
and Horseradish Crème Fraiche · 7.50

Warm Beet, Leek and Gorgonzola Bruschetta · 6.50

Linguine with Grilled Radicchio and Fennel
small · 6.00 large · 12.00

Creamy Saffron- Oyster Stew
with Sweet Peppers and Spinach · 7.50

Vegetarian Tapas with Olives and Pita Chips
Moroccan Eggplant Salad, Garden Beans with Dill and
Walnuts, Sherry Roasted Mushrooms
for two · 8.50

AN 18% GRATUITY WILL BE ADDED FOR
PARTIES OF 6 OR MORE

NO PIPE OR CIGAR SMOKING PLEASE

FORK
306 Market Street · Philadelphia, PA 19106 · 215. 625. 9425
October 15, 1997

Second Course

Greek Marinated Lamb Chop with Sautéed Spinach,
Couscous, Grilled Zucchini and Onions · 18.00

Grilled Rib Eye in Smoked Mushroom Demi- Glace
with Rosemary Roasted Potatoes
and Garlic Sautéed Greens · 17.50

Pan- Roasted, Free- Range Organic Lemon- Thyme
Chicken with Caramelized Onion Mashed Potatoes and
Sweet Corn Succotash · 14.50

Sautéed Pork Medallions and Apple- Brandy Sauce
with Pancetta- Braised Savoy Cabbage
and Roasted Turnips · 14.00

Pan- Seared Scallops in Tarragon Butter
and French Lentils with Bacon · 14.50

Peppery Grilled Tuna with Caper Vinaigrette over Sauté
of Garden Beans, Potatoes and Cherry Tomatoes · 16.00

Pan- Crisped, Honey- Soy Salmon with Gingered Sweet
Potatoes and Stir- Fried Vegetables · 16.00

Rosemary Roasted Halibut with Tomato- Potato Gratin
and Sautéed Kale · 14.50

Flaky Tart filled with Grilled Portobella, Tomato and
Smoked Mozzarella Cheese · 12.00

Sides

Caramelized Onion Mashed Potatoes · 3.50

Spinach with Garlic, Olive Oil and Lemon · 3.50

Sweet Corn Succotash · 3.50

Gingered Sweet Potatoes · 3.50

French Lentils with Bacon · 3.50

While some recipes cited here as Anne-Marie's were maintained in our files, some have been reconstructed from my memories of her cooking and no doubt vary significantly from her original recipes.

Roasting garlic brings out the sweetness in the garlic and removes some of its acidity. To roast garlic, preheat oven to 400°F. Place unpeeled garlic bulbs in ovenproof pan and then into oven. Bake 30 minutes. Squeeze garlic cloves out of their papery skins. Variations on this method include adding a little water or extra-virgin olive oil to the pan or wrapping garlic in aluminum foil before roasting.

Although a menu that changes daily sounds great theoretically, it can be stressful for everyone involved. The chef must always be thinking of fresh and inventive combinations that will leave guests wanting to come back. The waiters and cooks have to become familiar with the menu every day. And not all dishes sell at the same pace, so Anne-Marie had to predict how much of each dish to make and how much food to order. Sometimes we ran out of popular dishes, and sometimes people wanted a dish that was no longer being served. Over time, however, we established a steady flow of regulars who understood these challenges and liked having something new each time they came to Fork for a meal.

We did find that certain dishes were crowd pleasers, though, and we placed them on the menu fairly often. By the end of the second week, we knew that one of those dishes was Anne-Marie's Creamed Brussels Sprouts, which accompanied a succulent half of a pan-roasted, free-range chicken with mustard, sage and mashed potatoes with caramelized onions. These creamy sprouts have the power to change anyone's bad childhood memory of Brussels sprouts!

creamed brussels sprouts

Makes 4 to 6 side portions

4 T sweet butter

2 tsp minced garlic

Two 10-ounce cartons Brussels sprouts, coarsely shredded

1 tsp salt

½ tsp nutmeg

¼ tsp freshly ground black pepper

⅓ cup heavy cream

In a heavy sauté pan, melt butter over medium-high heat. Sauté garlic for 30 seconds. Add Brussels sprouts and salt. Cook 3 to 5 minutes, stirring frequently. Add nutmeg, pepper and cream. Stir well. Cook 2 minutes longer. Serve immediately.

Serve as an accompaniment to grilled chicken, pork or other meat.

Over the past ten years of Fork's menu, two of the dishes most frequently requested and even more popular than the Creamy Brussels Sprouts were Anne-Marie's creations. The first was Romaine Lettuce with Gorgonzola, Roasted Garlic–Honey Dressing and Spiced Pecans, which first made its appearance in November 1997. It was a variation of a Caesar salad, garnished with candied spiced pecans.

romaine lettuce with gorgonzola, roasted garlic–honey dressing and spiced pecans

Serves 8 as a dinner appetizer or 4 as a lunch entrée

ROASTED GARLIC–HONEY DRESSING

2 heads roasted garlic (see sidebar)

¾ cup olive oil

2 T Dijon mustard

⅓ cup honey

¼ cup apple cider vinegar

⅓ cup apple cider

salt and freshly ground black pepper to taste

Place garlic, Dijon mustard, honey, vinegar and cider in a food processor and process about 1 minute to purée garlic and combine ingredients. With motor running, slowly add reserved olive oil so that it emulsifies. Season with salt and pepper.

SPICED PECANS

2 quarts water

½ pound pecan halves

2 cups water

1 cup white sugar

1 tsp cayenne

1 tsp paprika

2 tsp ground allspice

peanut oil for frying

Bring water to a boil in a small saucepot. Blanch pecans for 2 minutes. Drain. Rinse with cold water and drain thoroughly.

Combine sugar and spices with 2 cups cold water in a small, heavy saucepot. Bring to boil, reduce heat and simmer for 2 to 3 minutes. Add pecans and cook 5 minutes. Drain.

Pour enough peanut oil into a heavy skillet to reach 3 inches. Using a candy thermometer to check the temperature, heat oil to 350°F. Add pecans and cook for 3 to 5 minutes,

until they are brown and crisp. Remove with a slotted spoon or Chinese strainer. Drain on paper towels. Cool and store in an airtight container. The nuts will keep for several days and are great for munching

SALAD

1 head romaine, washed

8 ounces Gorgonzola cheese, crumbled

8 to 12 ounces roasted garlic–honey dressing (recipe above)

½ pound spiced pecans

Rip romaine leaves into pieces. Toss with dressing and Gorgonzola cheese. Sprinkle with spiced pecans.

roasted chilean sea bass with dill pine-nut crust, chive mashed potatoes and sugar snap peas

Serves 6 as a dinner main course

DILL PINE-NUT CRUST

Can be made in advance

3 T olive oil

1 cup panko (Japanese breadcrumbs)

1 bunch fresh dill, cleaned
    and minced

½ bunch flat-leaf parsley, cleaned,
    destemmed and minced

½ cup pine nuts, toasted
    and crushed

salt and freshly ground black pepper
    to taste

Pulse breadcrumbs in a food processor several times to crush them further. Heat oil in a skillet over medium-high heat. Add breadcrumbs, stir to coat with oil and toast until the crumbs become golden in color, about 5 minutes. Transfer to a mixing bowl and allow them to cool slightly. Add remaining ingredients, mix thoroughly and set aside.

CHIVE MASHED POTATOES

8 Idaho russet potatoes, peeled
    and cut into large cubes

4 T butter

1 cup whole milk

2 T chopped chives

salt and freshly ground black pepper
    to taste

Place potatoes in a large pot. Add water to cover by 2 inches. Bring to a boil over high heat. Reduce heat and simmer until potatoes are fork tender, about 20 minutes. Meanwhile, melt butter into milk in a small saucepan over low heat. Drain potatoes in a colander. Return them to the pot. Add butter-and-milk mixture and mash potatoes with a sturdy whisk or potato masher. Add chives and salt and pepper to taste and whip potatoes briefly in a mixer or food processor. Set aside potatoes and keep warm.

BEURRE BLANC

1 cup white wine

¼ cup lemon juice

1 small shallot, chopped

1 T heavy cream

12 T (1½ sticks or 3 ounces)
    unsalted butter, chilled, cut into
    small pieces

salt and white pepper to taste

Combine shallots, white wine and lemon juice in a medium pan over medium-high heat and reduce liquid to about 2 tablespoons. Add cream and stir to combine. Reduce heat to low and begin whisking in butter, moving the pan on and off the heat as the butter slowly melts and the mixture becomes a smooth sauce. Season with white pepper and a pinch of sauce to taste. Strain (optional) and serve immediately, or store in a thermos until ready to use.

CHILEAN SEA BASS

Four 6-ounce Chilean sea-bass filets, rinsed and patted dry

2 T olive oil

Preheat oven to 375°F. Rub filets with olive oil and sprinkle both sides with salt and pepper. Position filets on a baking sheet and top each with about 2 tablespoons of crust. Roast filets in oven for about 10 minutes, just until the fish is moist and flakes easily.

SAUTÉED SUGAR SNAP PEAS

2 cups sugar snap peas, cleaned

1 clove garlic, minced

2 T olive oil

salt and freshly ground black pepper to taste

Heat olive oil in a large pan over medium-high heat. When oil is hot, add garlic and sauté about 10 seconds, stirring to avoid burning. Add sugar snap peas, lower heat to medium and sauté about 5 minutes, until peas are slightly tender but still crisp.

To serve, place a spoonful of mashed potatoes on the plate and snap peas to the side. Place fish crust-side up over snap peas. Lightly drizzle with beurre blanc. Serve immediately.

Chilean sea bass, also known as Patagonian toothfish, is a delicious, buttery deep-sea fish from Antarctica that has gained popularity over the past twenty years. We were one of the first restaurants to put Chilean sea bass on its menu, and we were one of the first to take it off; about two years after we started serving Chilean sea bass, it appeared on the list of overfished seafood.

Although not technically considered endangered in the United States, it is still considered an overfished species. Illegal fishing of this species increases the probability of its extinction. Cod, halibut or butterfish are good alternatives in recipes that call for Chilean sea bass.

Another of Anne-Marie's most popular creations was Roasted Chilean Sea Bass with Dill Pine-Nut Crust, Chive Mashed Potatoes and Sugar Snap Peas. My mother had steamed Chilean sea bass when she cooked for our family, but I hadn't seen the fish on many restaurant menus in Philadelphia. Our seafood purveyor brought it to Anne-Marie's attention as an affordable, delicious fish. When roasted, Chilean sea bass is very buttery, moist, flaky and hard to overcook. With it, Anne-Marie created the quintessential comfort food—a fish that melted in your mouth, accompanied by a rich, flavorful sauce and creamy mashed potatoes! Once this dish appeared on our menu, the most common dinner combination became the romaine salad as an appetizer and the Chilean sea bass as an entrée.

cooking for the seasons

Shad is indigenous to the East Coast and was fished for hundreds of years by Native Americans. At that time, shad was plentiful in rivers ranging from the southern tip of the United States all the way north to Canada. Like salmon, shad are born into rivers, swim out to sea and then return to rivers to spawn. The spawning period generally coincides with the spring and lasts about a month. There are shad fanatics who love fishing for and eating them, and shad festivals are held along rivers from the mid-Atlantic to New England.

The underlying success of Anne-Marie's cooking style, which ultimately became Fork's signature, was the quality and freshness of the ingredients. From the beginning, she carefully selected vendors who represented the best in their areas, many of whom she knew through the White Dog. To our benefit, most of these relationships continued to grow even after Anne-Marie moved on; for the most part, the same purveyors have served us over the past ten years.

Although some purveyors were larger, a handful—particularly the farmers—were small businesses like us. Even though there was a slight premium in price, Anne-Marie bought as much produce as possible from these local farmers. The quality and taste of their produce was superior to anything brought in from other areas. Whether they come to us from New Jersey or Pennsylvania, for instance, local heirloom tomatoes always taste better than their counterparts from South Carolina or hydroponically grown tomatoes. They taste like real tomatoes.

Our purveyors were as fond of Anne-Marie as she was of them. She was an extremely down-to-earth person. Whereas she rarely wanted to be in the dining room, schmoozing with guests, she felt at ease befriending many of the farmers. On occasional Mondays (when Fork was closed), she would even take our staff out for a picnic at Branch Creek Farm, an organic grower in nearby Bucks County, Pennsylvania, or for a swim at the goat-cheese-maker's pool in Chester County, a western suburb.

One benefit of working with local farmers is getting a great sense of what is available and tastes best during each season. During the spring, summer and early fall, when the farmers delivered weekly or biweekly, Anne-Marie's excitement at each delivery was contagious. We highlighted the farmers' ingredients on the menu to emphasize how fresh the food was. And over time our customers began to appreciate the arrival of particular ingredients nearly as much as we did.

SPRING

Spring, of course, was a season of excitement, as the range of available items began to expand. One of the first inklings that the menu was transitioning into spring was the introduction of shad. Anne-Marie was thrilled each spring when our fishmonger told her that shad was available.

In one of my favorite of Anne-Marie's shad preparations, she put a twist on the classic combination of shad, steamed new potatoes and asparagus. The only catch with shad is that it's extremely bony, so watch out!

broiled shad with peppery watercress sauce over steamed new potatoes, asparagus, peas and cherry tomatoes

Serves 6 as a dinner main course

PEPPERY WATERCRESS SAUCE

3 cups watercress, washed and patted dry

2 T lemon juice

1 tsp salt

¼ tsp pepper

½ cup extra-virgin olive oil

Combine 2 cups watercress, lemon juice, salt and pepper in bowl of food processor. Pulse until watercress is coarsely chopped. With processor running, add olive oil in a slow, steady stream, allowing the mixture to emulsify. Transfer to a mixing bowl. Coarsely chop remaining 1 cup watercress and stir into sauce.

BROILED SHAD

Six 6-ounce shad filets, de-boned

¼ cup olive oil

2 tsp fresh-squeezed lemon juice

salt and freshly ground black pepper to taste

bread crumbs

1 dozen new potatoes, blanched and halved

½ cup asparagus tips, blanched and cut into 2-inch pieces

½ cup English peas, hulled and shelled

10 cherry tomatoes, halved

Preheat broiler. Combine olive oil, lemon juice, salt and pepper to make a sauce. Place fish, skin side up, on an oiled broiler pan and brush with the sauce. Broil for 4 minutes, about 3 to 4 inches from heat. Carefully turn filets and brush other side with marinade.

Broil for an additional 4 to 5 minutes. While second side is broiling, heat 2 tablespoons olive oil in a hot pan. Mix potatoes, asparagus tips, English peas and tomatoes quickly in pan to heat through. Transfer to plate(s). When fish is lightly browned and flakes easily with a fork, use a spatula to move fish to each plate. Sprinkle with bread crumbs.

Mix watercress sauce to ensure that it is emulsified. Spoon on top of shad and vegetables. Garnish with parsley, lemon or watercress.

Judy Dornstreich, Branch Creek Farm

Another sure sign of spring was the appearance of local asparagus on the menu, usually in April or May. Although available year round, asparagus begins to lose its sweetness the moment it is cut. Asparagus goes nicely with most other spring vegetables, such as radishes, baby carrots and sweet peas. Since spring is also the season when wild salmon swim upstream to spawn, Anne-Marie developed this recipe for a spring luncheon; she liked the way the soft-green spring vegetables looked against the pink-orange salmon. Although at Fork we smoke our own salmon, you may find it more convenient to use one of the high-quality brands of smoked salmon. However, if you wish to smoke your own, it's easy to figure out how (see sidebar).

smoked salmon and spring vegetables in lemon-horseradish dressing

Serves 6 as an appetizer or 4 for a lunch entrée

LEMON-HORSERADISH DRESSING

1 shallot, minced

2 lemons (chopped zest and juice), approximately ½ cup

a pinch of sugar

2 T horseradish, drained

1 tsp salt

½ tsp freshly ground black pepper

1 cup canola or other vegetable oil

2 T chopped fresh dill

Combine shallot, lemon zest and juice and sugar in a small bowl. Allow to sit a few minutes so the sweetness of the shallot can develop. Add horseradish, salt and pepper. Whisking constantly, slowly add oil. Add dill and adjust seasoning as necessary to taste. Set aside as you prepare vegetables. This dressing will keep for several days in the refrigerator, although the bright green of the dill will darken.

SMOKED SALMON AND SPRING VEGETABLES

18 stalks of asparagus, snapped at the base and lightly blanched

6 radishes, sliced thin

18 baby carrots, peeled, trimmed and lightly blanched

½ cup shelled peas, lightly blanched

18 cherry tomatoes, halved if large

1 pound smoked salmon

freshly ground black pepper

a few snipped chives for garnish

crème fraîche, optional

Toss vegetables lightly with dressing. Arrange artfully on plates. Arrange smoked salmon on top of vegetables. Drizzle with a bit more dressing and sprinkle with black pepper and chives. Crème fraîche makes a nice accompaniment.

How to Smoke Salmon

At Fork and at home, I use a simple smoker that consists of two metal trays and a lid. (If the instructions for using your smoker differ from mine, please follow the instructions for your smoker.) This is how I use mine.

Place smoker over stove or grill and fill the bottom with your favorite type of wood chips. Place the salmon on the inner pan. Light stove or grill and bring heat to high under the smoker. Smoke salmon for about 10 minutes. Remove from heat and allow smoker to cool. To avoid filling your home with smoke, only open your smoker outside; do not open the smoker inside, even if you have a strong exhaust fan, or your house will fill with smoke.

peppery seared tuna with black-olive vinaigrette over green beans, new potatoes, fennel and cherry tomatoes

Serves 6 as a dinner main course or 8 as a lunch entrée

BLACK-OLIVE VINAIGRETTE

1 bunch parsley, cleaned and destemmed (about 1 cup of leaves)

1 scallion, chopped into 1-inch pieces

2 T chopped shallots

1 garlic clove, roughly chopped

¼ cup white-wine vinegar

1 cup Kalamata olives, pitted

juice of 1 lemon

⅛ tsp salt

1 cup extra-virgin olive oil

Combine parsley, scallion, shallots and garlic in bowl of food processor and pulse several times to chop roughly. Add vinegar, olives and lemon juice and pulse a few more times, chopping olives. With processor running, add olive oil in a slow, steady stream, allowing mixture to emulsify. Transfer to a container and set aside.

9 new potatoes, halved

½ pound green beans

1 fennel bulb, sliced

1 pint cherry tomatoes, halved

Fill a large pot with water, add potatoes and bring water to a boil. Reduce heat and simmer until potatoes are fork tender. Drain potatoes, return them to pot and cover to keep warm.

In a separate pot, bring several cups of water to a boil, season generously with salt, drop beans in and boil for 2 minutes, just until beans are tender but crisp and bright green. Drain, then mix with potatoes, fennel and tomatoes. When ready to serve, pour a half cup of vinaigrette on the vegetables and toss to coat.

PEPPERY SEARED TUNA

1 T white peppercorns, crushed

1 T black peppercorns, crushed

1 T coriander seeds, crushed

1 T anise

Six 6-ounce pieces ahi tuna loin, sushi grade

1 T olive oil

Place spices into a food processor or spice grinder and coarsely chop. Pour spices on a plate and lightly dust all sides of fish.

Heat olive oil in a large pan over high heat. When oil is hot but not burning, put tuna into pan and sear 1 minute on each side for rare.

To serve, place a large spoonful of warm vegetables tossed with vinaigrette on each plate, top with tuna and garnish with baby greens. Drizzle with additional dressing.

It's not that Anne-Marie was partial to fish, but adding it seemed a natural way to lighten the menu after a winter of hearty meals. Salads, too, were particularly welcome in spring. The classic spring Salade Niçoise was another recipe to which Anne-Marie added her own twist. Instead of poached tuna, she would use *ahi* (sushi-grade tuna) or yellow-fin tuna, which she crusted in peppercorns and grilled. For those who love sushi, there is no other way to cook tuna but rare! She served it over a warm salad of potatoes, *haricots verts* (French green beans) or Branch Creek Farm garden beans and cherry tomatoes. Instead of merely throwing in a few olives, she created a vinaigrette from Greek Kalamata olives to make the dish even more flavorful. From time to time, Anne-Marie would change from tuna to swordfish or throw in pasta to make the dish a little different.

SUMMER

Summer in Anne-Marie's kitchen was a joyous time, full of fresh and beautiful foods coaxed into surprising combinations. One of her most popular summer dishes was a spinach salad with corn and goat cheese dressing. Although more than five years have passed since I've eaten this salad, I can almost taste the fresh, sweet corn that Anne-Marie cut off the cob to put into it. The goat cheese was local—Greystone Nubian's fresh chèvratel, made by Doug Newboldt, who had been a chef at the Frog Commissary, a major Philadelphia restaurant institution in the 1970's. Doug had left restaurant cooking to make cheese from her farm in Malvern, Chester County, just forty-five minutes west of Philadelphia. She kept her production very limited; now she only has about nine goats and distributes her cheese exclusively to the White Dog Cafe. I miss the young, fresh, citrusy taste of her goat cheese, which made a creamy dressing that was so delicious! We substituted Montrachet, but there are many terrific artisanal goat cheeses from American producers to try. This dressing recipe is almost a take on blue-cheese dressing, because its taste is so rich and creamy.

To emulsify means to mix two ingredients that don't ordinarily mix well, such as oil and vinegar. This is done by slowly adding one ingredient to the other and whisking briskly. Almost all sauces contain some kind of an emulsion. There are two kinds of emulsions, stable and unstable. An emulsion can be stabilized by the addition of mustard, egg yolks or another binding ingredient. Mayonnaise is a perfect example of a stabilized emulsion, while most vinaigrettes are unstable emulsions.

spinach salad with roasted crimini mushrooms, grilled vidalia onions, crispy pancetta and roasted corn with goat cheese dressing

Serves 4 to 6 as a dinner appetizer or 2 to 3 as a lunch entrée

GOAT CHEESE DRESSING

1½ cups (6 ounces) goat cheese, crumbled

½ cup olive oil

2 T lemon juice

salt and freshly ground black pepper to taste

Combine all ingredients in a blender.

SPINACH SALAD

8 ounces crimini mushrooms

1 large Vidalia onion, sliced into rings

4 ounces pancetta, diced small

kernels cut from 2 corn cobs

salt and freshly ground black pepper to taste

4 T olive oil

baby spinach

Preheat oven to 350°F. In a bowl, lightly coat crimini mushrooms in 2 tablespoons olive oil, ½ teaspoon salt and freshly ground black pepper. Transfer mushrooms to a baking pan and roast for 15 minutes. Remove from oven and transfer to a large bowl, reserving baking pan and juices. Set aside.

Toss onion rings in 2 tablespoons olive oil, ½ teaspoon salt and freshly ground black pepper. Grill rings on a hot grill or grill pan for approximately 10 minutes or until onions become tender and are slightly scorched.

Meanwhile, add corn kernels to the mushroom baking pan, toss in juices and roast for 5 minutes.

While onions grill, cook pancetta in a large skillet over medium-high heat until it is crispy. Drain on paper towel and set aside.

Combine mushrooms, corn, onions and pancetta. Season with additional salt and pepper. Toss with spinach and goat cheese dressing and serve.

Former dining room manager Megan Cave preparing for her shift

Of course Anne-Marie made ample use of summer herbs. She would get fresh marjoram from Branch Creek Farm. Marjoram, although part of the oregano family, is less sweet than oregano and has a slightly minty and citrusy flavor. This soup, characterized by marjoram's subtle taste, can be served hot or cold. If you prefer, you can substitute thyme or sage.

roasted pepper and corn soup

Serves 4 to 6

4 T butter

1 white onion, diced

2 red bell peppers, seeded and diced

4 ears sweet corn, cut off the cob

1 clove garlic, minced

½ cup flour

5 cups chicken stock

2 cups half and half

1 T chopped fresh marjoram, thyme
    or sage

salt and freshly ground black pepper
    to taste

In medium-heavy saucepot, melt butter. Add onion and red pepper and cook over medium-high heat for about 20 minutes, until onions and peppers start to brown. Add corn and garlic and cook another 5 minutes. Add flour and stir to combine. Cook 3 to 5 minutes, stirring often.

Add chicken stock and whisk to mix in flour and eliminate lumps. Bring to a boil. The mixture will thicken at this point. Reduce heat and simmer 5 minutes. Add half and half and simmer another 5 minutes. Purée in batches in food processor or blender. Return to pot. Add marjoram and season with salt and pepper.

Roberto's family heritage is Italian, and I have learned a lot about Italian cooking from his dinner parties and from our travels together in Italy. One of Italy's most classic culinary combinations is black mission figs and prosciutto, a cured Italian ham. The prosciutto should be sliced thin; if it's too thick, the dish will be too salty. The fattiness of the ham is offset by the sweetness of the figs, which are one of the most memorable fruits of summer. Anne-Marie would add baby farm greens to the plate and dress them in a slightly sweet rosemary-honey dressing. The pièces de résistance, however, were two or three buttery, cheesy pecorino crackers that she made from scratch. Roberto would always request an extra plate of crackers whenever he ordered this dish.

fresh figs with prosciutto, pecorino crackers and rosemary-honey dressing

Serves 4 to 6 as a dinner appetizer or 2 to 3 as a lunch entrée

ROSEMARY-HONEY DRESSING

1 T finely minced rosemary

1 T honey

2 T white balsamic vinegar

1/3 cup olive oil

Whisk together rosemary, honey and vinegar. Add olive oil in a slow stream, whisking vigorously to bring the mixture together.

PECORINO CRACKERS

1 stick of butter (½ cup or 4 ounces)

½ cup freshly grated pecorino Romano cheese

¾ cup all-purpose flour

Cream butter in a stand mixer with a paddle attachment on medium speed. Add cheese and continue to beat with paddle until butter becomes light in color and fluffy. Add flour in thirds, beating on low speed just until flour mixes into butter. Form dough into a log about 5 inches long and 2 inches thick. Wrap it in a sheet of plastic wrap and refrigerate for 2 hours or overnight.

When ready to bake crackers, preheat oven to 375°F. Unwrap dough and slice log into ¼-inch-thick rounds. Transfer to a baking sheet and bake for 15 to 20 minutes. Remove from oven and gently transfer to a wire rack to cool.

1 pint black mission figs, halved

¼ pound prosciutto di Parma, sliced thin

arugula or baby greens

Arrange thin slices of prosciutto on the plate. Toss arugula with Rosemary-Honey dressing (if using baby greens, drizzle dressing if greens are too delicate). Place to the side of the prosciutto. Arrange figs and crackers.

Moroccan couscous is a North African pasta made of the hard part of the wheat grain called semolina. To make couscous, the semolina is husked and crushed, but not ground. Moroccan couscous has a granular texture and is prepared by steaming. Israeli couscous, which we also use at the restaurant, is a larger version, more like pearl pasta.

Being the host of the restaurant, I find it difficult to eat at a decent time. Particularly during the summer, I often don't sit down to dinner before 9:30 P.M. In our early days, I found this dish the perfect late-night meal. Anne-Marie would make the snapper so that the skin was nice and crispy but the meat itself was still moist. The gazpacho vinaigrette captures all of the flavors of late summer, including tomatoes, cucumbers, jicama, peppers, onions and cilantro. A little Tabasco gives the dish a kick, and mustard greens add additional spiciness.

pan-crisped red snapper with gazpacho vinaigrette, herbed couscous and mustard greens

Serves 4 as a dinner main course

GAZPACHO VINAIGRETTE

1 large, ripe tomato, diced small

1 cucumber, peeled, seeded and diced small

½ small jicama, peeled and diced small (optional)

½ bunch scallions, sliced thin

1 yellow bell pepper, diced small

1 green bell pepper, diced small

1 T chopped fresh basil

1 T chopped fresh cilantro

1 cup tomato juice

½ cup orange juice

¼ cup sherry vinegar

¼ cup olive oil

1½ tsp Tabasco

1 tsp salt

Mix all ingredients together. Set aside.

HERBED COUSCOUS

10 ounces (about 1½ cups) Moroccan couscous

2 cups boiling water

1 tsp salt

½ cup flat-leaf parsley, chopped

½ cup fresh dill, chopped

½ cup sliced scallions

½ cup extra-virgin olive oil

freshly ground black pepper to taste

Place couscous in a large bowl. Add water and salt and stir to mix ingredients. Cover with plastic wrap to seal in the steam. Let sit for 5 minutes. Fluff with a fork to separate the grains. Add parsley, dill, scallions and olive oil. Mix and season with additional salt and pepper to taste.

MUSTARD GREENS

2 cups mustard greens, cleaned

1 clove garlic, minced

1 T olive oil

salt and freshly ground black pepper to taste

Heat oil in pan. When hot, add garlic. Reduce heat if necessary so as not to burn garlic. Add mustard greens and cook until they are wilted.

PAN-CRISPED RED SNAPPER

4 red snapper filets, approximately 6 ounces each

olive oil

salt and freshly ground black pepper to taste

Heat pan. When hot, add olive oil and sear fish with skin side up for about 3 minutes. Flip over and continue cooking until desired doneness (approximately 4 minutes for medium rare). To serve, place couscous and mustard greens on each plate. Position fish over couscous and greens. Spoon a generous amount of gazpacho vinaigrette over fish. Serve immediately.

Nothing at Fork is thrown away unless it absolutely cannot be used. Scraps of onions, carrots, celery and herbs are used to make chicken, vegetable, fish or meat stock, the base for all our cooked sauces. Running a kitchen efficiently means knowing how to use these little bits and pieces. In addition, being able to make use of a surfeit of a particular item is a challenge that the efficient cook must master. In the summertime especially, certain items are particularly abundant. When you buy them from local farmers, you can end up with bushels. Anne-Marie created this recipe as a way to utilize some of the vegetables that are particularly abundant in late summer—zucchini, squash, eggplant and tomatoes. The extra vinaigrette will keep for several days in the refrigerator and can also be used as a dip for crudités or pita or as a sauce for grilled chicken or pasta salad.

Fork wait staff, 2000

spinach salad with roasted summer-vegetable vinaigrette

Serves 4 to 6 as a dinner appetizer or 2 to 3 as a lunch entrée

ROASTED SUMMER-VEGETABLE VINAIGRETTE

1 medium zucchini

1 red bell pepper

½ green bell pepper

½ small eggplant

1 medium white onion

5 plum tomatoes

2 T minced garlic

¼ cup olive oil

2 T chopped fresh basil

1 cup tomato juice

1 T tomato paste

½ cup red wine vinegar

1½ cup olive oil

salt and freshly ground black pepper
to taste

Preheat oven to 400°F. Cut all vegetables to 1-inch size. Toss with ¼ cup olive oil and garlic. Place in a single layer in a roasting pan and roast about 15 minutes, until vegetables start to brown at edges. Let cool. Purée vegetables in blender or food processor. Remove purée to a large bowl. Add basil, tomato juice, tomato paste and vinegar. Whisking constantly, add olive oil slowly to emulsify. Season with salt and pepper.

SPINACH SALAD

2 bunches of spinach, washed
and destemmed

1 yellow pepper, julienned or cut into
¾-inch chunks

½ red onion, julienned

¼ pound Kalamata olives, pitted or
not, depending on your preference

12 ounces roasted summer-vegetable
vinaigrette

crumbled cheese (optional; use goat
or feta)

croutons

Toss all ingredients together and arrange on plates. At Fork, we make croutons from day-old bread, which we toss with olive oil, rosemary, salt and pepper and cook in the oven at a low temperature until they are crisp.

Late summer has its own flavors. This recipe always reminds me of September because it was on our opening menu and was placed consistently on the late-summer menu thereafter. The recipe was created by Anne-Marie's mother. Anne-Marie kept it top secret until she was finally persuaded to release it through a magazine somewhere. The surprise ingredient is anchovies, which Anne-Marie feared might deter people from ordering it. But the lamb was so tender and delicious that no one flinched, even after learning that there were cured anchovies in the marinade. We used loin lamb chops, which are a little fattier but a little less expensive than those from the rack. They were very succulent. You could serve them with couscous and wilted spinach or with grilled zucchini and our White-Bean Fennel Salad.

marinated greek lamb chops with grilled zucchini and white-bean fennel salad

Serves 4 as a dinner main course

MARINADE

8 anchovy filets

2 T Dijon mustard

2 cloves garlic, chopped

2 tsp dried Greek oregano

½ tsp chopped fresh rosemary
   (woody stem removed)

4 tsp lemon juice

2 T olive oil

½ tsp freshly ground black pepper

½ tsp Kosher salt

Combine all ingredients in food processor. Process 30 seconds.

LAMB CHOPS

8 to 10 loin lamb chops,
   4 to 5 ounces each

Coat lamb chops with marinade. Allow lamb to marinate 2 hours or overnight. Prepare grill. Grill for 4 to 6 minutes on each side for rare to medium-rare chops.

WHITE-BEAN FENNEL SALAD

2 cups dried white beans

3 garlic cloves

1 sprig of rosemary

½ medium red onion, halved
   and sliced very thin

1 fennel bulb, quartered and cubed

1 bunch parsley, chopped fine

½ cup olive oil

⅓ cup freshly squeezed lemon juice

zest of 1 lemon

1 tsp Kosher salt

freshly ground black pepper

Soak beans, using either the quick-soak or the overnight method (see sidebar). Drain beans and transfer to a large pot. Cover with water by 2 inches. Bring water to a boil, then reduce to a simmer. Add 2 garlic cloves, halved, and rosemary to the pot. Cover and simmer for about 1 hour, until beans are tender. Season beans with about 2 teaspoons of salt after 45 minutes of simmering.

While beans cook, mince remaining clove of garlic and crush it into a paste by sprinkling coarse salt on it and running the flat side of a knife across it. Whisk together garlic paste, salt, pepper and lemon juice. Add olive oil in a slow stream, whisking to incorporate.

When beans are tender, drain, remove garlic and rosemary, transfer to a bowl and let cool slightly. Toss beans with fennel, onion and parsley.

Pour olive oil and lemon mixture over salad and stir to coat. Adjust seasonings to taste.

GRILLED ZUCCHINI

2 zucchini (about 1½ pounds)

1 tsp Kosher salt

1 garlic clove, crushed into paste

¼ cup olive oil

freshly ground black pepper

Preheat grill to medium heat (or place a grill pan over medium-high heat). Slice zucchini lengthwise into ⅛-inch strips (use a slicer or mandoline for clean, even slices).

Whisk together salt, garlic paste and olive oil. Brush both sides of zucchini slices with oil mixture and sprinkle with freshly ground black pepper. Place zucchini strips diagonally across grates and grill approximately 2 minutes per side. Remove from grill.

To assemble, place about ½ cup of White-Bean Fennel Salad on each plate. Place grilled zucchini slices to the side. Arrange lamb chops over beans and zucchini. Drizzle extra-virgin olive oil over the top if desired. Garnish with rosemary or baby greens.

This is another recipe that uses up leftover August vegetables easily and without making them seem like leftovers. It would make a nice light lunch if served aside salad greens, or—cut smaller—could be used as a side for grilled chicken, fish or meat.

summer garden-vegetable gratin

Serves 4 to 6 as a lunch entrée

One 1 to 1½-pound medium eggplant

½ tsp salt

2 medium zucchinis, approximately 1 pound in total, cut into slices about ¼-inch thick

1 large white onion, peeled and sliced ⅛-inch thick

3 medium farm tomatoes, approximately 2 pounds

2 yellow peppers, seeded and julienned

¼ cup chopped fresh herbs (such as basil, oregano, parsley and sage)

1 cup olive oil

2 tsp Kosher salt

12 tsp freshly ground black pepper

2 T minced garlic

½ cup parmesan cheese (set aside ¼ cup for top of gratin)

Preheat oven to 400°F. Coat 2-quart, shallow casserole dish with olive oil.

Peel eggplant and slice into ¼-inch circles. Toss with ½ teaspoon salt. Set aside for 15 minutes while you prepare other vegetables. Rinse eggplant with water and pat dry with paper towels.

Have all ingredients handy to assemble the gratin.

Arrange a single layer of eggplant slices in bottom of casserole and sprinkle with a small amount of salt, pepper, herbs, garlic, cheese and olive oil. Repeat this process between every layer. Top eggplant with a layer of tomatoes, ½ of the sliced onion, and ½ of the julienned peppers. Next, layer the zucchini slices. Follow with more tomatoes, onions and peppers. Finally, top off with eggplant slices and a last sprinkling of seasonings. The layered vegetables will probably rise higher than the sides of the pan.

Coat a sheet of aluminum foil with olive oil and tightly cover casserole dish. Set on middle rack of oven with a baking sheet below it to catch any juices. Bake for 1 hour. Remove aluminum foil. Bake 10 more minutes. Sprinkle with remaining ¼ cup parmesan and bake 5 more minutes, until the cheese is melted and bubbly. Serve warm or at room temperature.

Dried beans Although dried beans are more time consuming to prepare, they are also more texturally pleasant and flavorful than their canned counterparts. Dried beans can be prepared using either the overnight or the quick-soak method. The overnight method simply requires soaking dried beans overnight in cold water. The quick-soak method speeds the process and ensures that the beans are not oversoaked, which can lead to a loss of flavor. To use this method, place dried beans in a pot and cover with at least 1 inch water. Bring water to a boil, reduce heat and simmer for approximately 2 minutes. Remove pot from heat, cover and let stand 1 hour. Drain beans and proceed with recipe.

Use approximately 12 cups of water per pound of dried beans for cooking. Cooking time will vary with the type of bean, but the larger the bean, the longer it takes to cook. Cooked beans should be tender, not mushy. The best way to tell if beans are cooked is to break one open. If there is no white center and the bean is close to the same color all the way through, it is cooked.

Roasting beets is easy. Just follow these instructions.

Preheat oven to 350°F. Wash beets and cut off their tops. Place beets in roasting pan and cover with water. Cover pan with foil and roast in oven for about 1 hour or until beets are fork tender. Allow them to cool in liquid. When they are cool, remove their peels, using your fingers or a paring knife. Beets can be prepared up to 2 days in advance and stored in the refrigerator.

FALL

The transition between summer and fall is always exciting in the kitchen. Harvest time brings an end to late-summer vegetables and ushers in the squashes and root vegetables of early fall. Beets are always abundant at this time. Although beets are in vogue now, when Fork opened they were not popular on restaurant menus. The only ones I knew of were the pickled kind available in jars in supermarkets. Normally I am open-minded about food, but I had never tried beets because I always felt there was something artificial about the color and juice of those pickled ones. Then Anne-Marie introduced me to fresh, roasted beets the first time she cooked for Roberto and me at his home. I've been hooked on beets ever since. This recipe is a great way to make use of day-old bread. The earthy flavor of the beets makes an excellent pair with Gorgonzola.

beet, leek and gorgonzola bruschetta

Makes 6 to 8 bruschetta

2 to 3 medium-to-large beets, red or yellow, roasted, cut into ¼-inch cubes

2 leeks, halved, sliced thin and cleaned

2 T extra-virgin olive oil

1 T unsalted butter

salt and freshly ground black pepper

¼ pound Italian Gorgonzola, crumbled (use *dolce* for a younger, sweeter cheese or *piccante* for a saltier, more pungent cheese)

1 day-old baguette or other fresh, country-style bread, sliced ½-inch thick on a bias

¼ cup olive oil

Melt butter into olive oil in a large pan over medium-high heat. Add leeks and sauté until translucent, about 4 minutes. Season with salt and pepper to taste.

Preheat broiler. Place slices of bread on a tray, generously brush with olive oil and season with salt and pepper. Lightly toast under the broiler for 2 minutes. Flip toasted slices over, spread a tablespoon of leeks on top, and top with roasted beets and a sprinkle of crumbled Gorgonzola. Return toasts to the oven until cheese is melted, 1 to 2 minutes. Serve with a side of salad or baby greens.

This is another salad that always reminds me of fall. In 1998, Anne-Marie was invited to be the featured chef for a luncheon at the James Beard House in New York City. This is a prestigious honor, a trek all young chefs want to make, almost like a debutante's coming-out party. The James Beard House, originally the home of the late chef, showcases culinary artists from around the world. Chefs, winemakers and cookbook authors are invited to prepare a special meal for members of the James Beard Foundation and the culinary community. One of the courses she made for the luncheon was this salad, which was one of her signature dishes. Fresh figs in the vinaigrette add a slightly sweet, fruity flavor to the salad. Again, we used Doug Newboldt's goat cheese; however, any fresh goat cheese is delicious. The prosciutto must be sliced thin and should be warmed just enough to melt the goat cheese.

warm chèvre wrapped in prosciutto over spinach with fig vinaigrette and toasted hazelnuts

Serves 4 as a dinner appetizer or 2 to 3 as a lunch entrée

FIG VINAIGRETTE

4 fresh figs, cleaned, stems removed, cut into quarters

¼ cup white balsamic vinegar

2 T water

1 T honey

1 tsp lemon juice

½ cup olive oil

Combine water and balsamic vinegar in a small saucepan. Add figs and bring mixture to a simmer. Reduce heat and let figs steep for 10 minutes. Transfer to a blender, then add honey and lemon juice and purée. With blender running, add oil in a slow, steady stream and process until ingredients are combined.

WARM CHÈVRE WRAPPED IN PROSCIUTTO OVER SPINACH

one 4- to 6-ounce log of chèvre, sliced into ¼-inch disks

¼ pound prosciutto di Parma, sliced paper thin

2 T toasted hazelnuts, chopped

8 ounces baby spinach, cleaned and spun dry

Preheat oven to 375°F. Cut prosciutto slices in half so each is about 3 inches long. Place a cheese disk on top of one piece of prosciutto and fold up the four sides around the cheese and over each other to close.

If prosciutto slices are too big, trim them down into a rectangular shape to make it easier to tuck ends together. Repeat this process with each chèvre disk. Place the wrapped cheese on a baking sheet lined with foil and transfer to oven. Bake just until cheese is warmed through, about 5 minutes.

Toss spinach with 1 or 2 tablespoons vinaigrette and arrange a small pile on each plate. Prop one prosciutto-wrapped chèvre medallion against the side of each mound of spinach. Sprinkle with toasted hazelnuts and drizzle with additional vinaigrette, if desired.

As the weather got chillier, Anne-Marie's soups became popular. Some guests requested to be called whenever a certain soup appeared on the menu. Although this soup has a creamy texture, it is vegan! The coconut milk, ginger and lemongrass impart an extremely exotic flavor. I could probably eat this with basmati rice for days and be happy.

sweet-potato lemongrass soup

Serves 4 to 6

3 T vegetable oil

1 large white onion, diced

2-inch piece of ginger, peeled and minced

1 jalapeño, seeded and minced

4 cloves garlic, peeled and minced

3 pounds sweet potatoes (approximately 5 large potatoes), peeled and sliced ½-inch thick

7 cups water

10 stalks lemongrass, outer dry leaves removed and bulb-like base crushed

7 ounces coconut milk

salt and freshly ground black pepper to taste

chives for garnish

In a large, heavy saucepot, heat oil over medium-high heat. Add onion and sauté until translucent (about 5 minutes). Add ginger, jalapeño and garlic. Sauté another 2 minutes. Add sweet potatoes and water to the pot. There should be just enough water to cover the sweet potatoes. Tie stalks of lemongrass together with string and put base end of stalks into soup. Bring liquid to a boil, reduce heat and allow liquid to simmer. Cook about 15 minutes, until potatoes break apart. Remove from heat.

Discard lemongrass stalks. Purée soup in batches in food processor or blender. Strain through a sieve. Stir in coconut milk; season with salt and pepper. Garnish with chives.

Lemongrass is an Indian herb used in Asian and Caribbean cooking. Lemongrass is very pungent, so only a small amount need be used. Its light, lemony flavor blends well with garlic, chilies and fresh cilantro.

To release the flavor, flatten the bulb with the flat end of a chef's knife or pound it with a mallet. Lemongrass is fibrous, so strain the liquid in which it was cooked before serving.

Since opening Fork, Roberto and I have almost always had dinner together on Sunday nights. This tradition began because we needed to taste the many wines that vendors drop off for consideration for the wine list. As Roberto likes to say, "It's a tough job, but someone's got to do it." As Fork's wine director, Roberto believes that the wines should be tasted independently, without the influence of salespeople. He tastes these wines on Sunday nights, not when salespeople stop by to drop off their wares. All potential wines are judged against other wines of like varietals or style and evaluated for balance, taste, value and possible position on the wine list. This is frustrating to many wine representatives, who often want to know more about the elusive Roberto Sella.

From day one, we have tried to create our wine list based on quality, not quantity. We never add a wine simply to fill out the list. Our opening wine list offered six to eight whites and an equal number of reds. Since the size of the list was limited, one of the challenges Roberto faced was educating the waitstaff about wine varietals that were unfamiliar to them, as well as about how to pair the wines with food. Despite their many years of experience (we used to joke that our waitstaff had over a hundred years of cumulative experience), our waitstaff had been exposed primarily to chardonnay and cabernet. Additionally, none of the wines on our list offered brand recognition. This was by design. Because we operate in the Commonwealth of Pennsylvania under a rigid regulatory system in which consumers pay the exact same price as restaurants do for liquor, we decided to select wines that were not readily available to consumers in Pennsylvania and that offered great value.

But at first, our wine list created battles with the staff. Our servers had a feeling of ownership toward the restaurant and took it personally if a guest wasn't happy, regardless of the reason. So when guests were unhappy because our wine list did not include many recognizable or popular California wines, the staff fought to alter the list to include more of these wines.

Although Roberto refused to simplify the list, he would go out of his way to satisfy a particular customer. I remember one night when two women came in and ordered a bottle of red wine. Their waiter called me over to tell me that these two women thought our wine list "sucked." Roberto just happened to walk into the restaurant at that moment, so I sent him over to the table to speak with them. Roberto says he felt ambushed by the women. But Roberto never loses his composure. He asked them calmly to describe the type of wine they liked and what their ideal wine would be for their dinner. Then he told them that if they could wait just fifteen minutes, he would produce the wine they desired. Unbeknownst to me and the two women, Roberto left the restaurant, got in a cab, went home and returned with a fabulous bottle of red zinfandel from a prestigious California producer. After tasting the wine, the guests told Roberto that this was exactly the style of wine they had wanted and asked where it was on the list. He explained to them that he had brought them a complimentary bottle from his personal wine cellar. The two women left ecstatic.

WINTER

In the wintertime, everyone craves comfort food, especially when coming in from the cold. Brunch is the ultimate winter comfort meal, and it was also Anne-Marie's baby. From the scent of freshly baked muffins to the savory smell of bacon wafting through the dining room, her cooking created an irresistible atmosphere on Sunday mornings. All the muffins, coffee cake and sticky buns were baked that morning. Even the granola was handmade from oats, honey and nuts. Because I work in a restaurant and am always surrounded by temptation, I have to be very careful about what I eat, and maintaining my willpower during brunch is not an easy feat. For the most part I succeed, but at least once a year I indulge in the cheddar grits. Often, Anne-Marie's grits were served with spicy shrimp, sautéed peppers and onions, but you could also serve them with any sort of well-seasoned fish, meat, pork or poultry.

Sautéed Brussels sprouts, perfect as the weather cools down

fork cheddar grits

Makes 4 side servings

½ medium onion, diced

1 cup half and half

1 cup heavy cream

½ cup dried grits

⅓ cup grated cheddar

salt and freshly ground black pepper to taste

1 T butter

Melt butter in a medium pot over moderate heat. Add onions and sauté until soft. Add cream and half and half. Bring to a boil. Stir in grits. Reduce heat and simmer for about 10 minutes, stirring frequently. Add cheese and mix to melt it. Season with salt and pepper to taste.

In the wintertime, we can't fill our entire menu with local ingredients. But our farmers offer plenty of root vegetables, such as parsnips, turnips and celery root, so we make use of these ingredients regularly. This recipe was a creative way to put a spin on root vegetables. Caraway is an unusual spice, but you could easily substitute freshly chopped herbs such as rosemary, thyme or sage, or even cumin seeds, coriander seeds or Madras curry.

roasted winter vegetables with caraway

Makes 8 side portions

2 large carrots, approximately
   1 pound, peeled

2 parsnips, approximately
   ½ pound, peeled

1 celery root, approximately
   1 pound, peeled

2 large turnips, approximately
   ¾ pound

3 Yukon gold potatoes, approximately
   ¾ pound

1 white onion

10 Brussels sprouts

20 medium crimini mushrooms

2 tsp caraway seeds, ground coarse

2 tsp Kosher salt

2 tsp freshly ground black pepper

6 T olive oil

Preheat oven to 400°F. Cut carrots, parsnips, celery root, turnips, potatoes and onion into ¾ inch chunks, keeping each type of vegetable apart from the others. Trim bases of Brussels sprouts and cut in half. Wipe mushrooms free of dirt.

On a cookie sheet, toss carrots and parsnips with ½ teaspoon caraway, ½ teaspoon salt, ½ teaspoon pepper and 4 teaspoons olive oil. Spread out. Repeat with three other mixtures: celery root and potatoes, Brussels sprouts and turnips, and mushrooms and onions. Use a separate cookie sheet for each mixture.

Put cookie sheets in preheated oven and roast vegetables for 10 to 15 minutes. Cooking times will vary because of vegetable textures and dicing sizes. The best way to tell if the vegetables are done is to put a fork into them and make sure they are cooked through. Mix vegetables together and serve immediately.

I like duck best in winter, as cooler weather puts me in the mood for gamey meats. Duck has always been an extremely popular entrée at Fork. Many people like the meaty, tender consistency of duck breast. The lentil pilaf in this recipe offers a nice alternative to potatoes.

pan-seared duck breasts with green-peppercorn glaze atop lentil-rice pilaf

Serves 4 as a dinner main course

GREEN-PEPPERCORN GLAZE

1 tsp green peppercorns, crushed

1 cup red wine

1 shallot, minced

1 bay leaf

1 cup veal or duck *demi-glace* (see recipe in Fork Foundations or use store-bought)

½ tsp honey

Combine green peppercorns, shallot, bay leaf and red wine in small saucepot. Reduce to ¼ cup over medium heat. Add demi-glace and reduce over medium-high heat until thickened. Remove bay leaf and stir in honey. Set aside in a warm place.

VINAIGRETTE

2 T red-wine vinegar

2 tsp Dijon mustard

1 tsp chopped fresh thyme

5 T olive oil

salt and freshly ground black pepper to taste

Combine vinegar, mustard and thyme in a small bowl. Whisking constantly, slowly add olive oil. Emulsify. Season with salt and pepper. Set aside.

LENTIL-RICE PILAF

2 cups cooked French lentils

2 cups cooked wild rice

1 scallion, sliced thin

1 small carrot, diced

1 stalk celery, diced

1 T olive oil

In large sauté pan, heat olive oil. Add vegetables and cook briefly over medium heat. Add lentils and wild rice and stir to heat. Remove from heat and dress with vinaigrette. Set aside in a warm place.

PAN-SEARED DUCK BREASTS

4 duck breasts, fat scored

2 T olive oil

Heat oil in heavy sauté pan. Sear duck to desired temperature. Slice thin. Serve with pilaf and Green-Peppercorn Glaze. Sautéed Swiss chard is a nice accompaniment.

How to Pan Sear Duck Breast

Duck breast is best when it is cooked medium rare and has a crispy skin. Rendering the thick layer of fat that lies between the skin and the breast meat results in wonderfully crispy skin. To render, first score fat with a sharp knife in a crosshatch pattern, taking care not to cut through meat. Place duck breast skin-side down in a hot pan over medium-high heat. Sear skin for 1 to 2 minutes, then reduce heat to low and cook slowly, melting away fat layer. Continue cooking for about 15 minutes. Turn meat over for an additional 2 minutes or until meat is medium rare.

As I mentioned earlier, to be successful, a restaurant must have a clear, concise and consistent vision. We started out applying this principle to food, but soon Anne-Marie was rolling full steam ahead. She was extremely capable and ran the kitchen efficiently, without needing much help. Thus I began to spend most of my time developing a service vision.

Good service is as important as good food. Yet as with food, the definition of good service is extremely subjective. Maybe I have read too many business-school textbooks, but I have always felt that good service means exceeding your customer's expectations on multiple levels. In the restaurant business, that means making sure that every guest leaves delighted by his or her meal, the restaurant's ambience and the staff's hospitality. Diners should feel that the staff is friendly and accommodating, from the time they make their reservation to the end of their meal. And servers need to be familiar enough with the menu to be able to answer all sorts of questions, including questions relating to food allergies, requests for substitutions and other special concerns.

Perhaps coordinating a service team sounds simple, but achieving a perfect night at a restaurant is virtually impossible. Changes in reservations, timing of guests' arrivals, traffic, readiness of the kitchen staff and waitstaff, temperaments of the staff and guests and the actual menu selections can all influence the flow of service during the evening.

"Flow of service" refers to the tempo of the meal. That tempo is thrown off if a guest has to wait too long to order, or if there are delays between courses. Then the guest perceives the meal as occurring at a pace that is too fast or too slow. Achieving an even flow is every host's aim.

Thien, our current chef, once said to me that the staff members at the front and the back of the house are there to support each other, because both teams rarely operate at the same time without any breaks in flow. When the food is outstanding, the service might be off, but the excellent food can help compensate; and when the kitchen is not running smoothly, the quality of service can outshine whatever flaws might exist in the meal.

When I set out to define our service vision and build our waitstaff, I recognized how important it is to have a pleasant, gracious and intelligent team. I knew, too, that a vital component of customer service is being able to handle complaints, big and small, to a customer's satisfaction. Thus my plan was to hire experienced servers who would give great service and to empower them to resolve customer complaints on the spot. The most common reason servers give for changing jobs is a lack of respect from management; they simply don't believe that their opinions are valued. With this thought in mind, I set out to find servers who would gain a sense of ownership in the restaurant by participating in our decision-making processes.

Initially, we recruited staff by word of mouth, since we didn't have the budget to advertise. My first hire was Karen Gibson, an artist who had recently worked at the Rose Tattoo Restaurant. The owners of the Rose, Michael and Helene

Weinstein, who helped me review my initial plans, were exceptional at identifying good staff. Anyone I have ever known or hired who has the Rose Tattoo on his or her résumé has been hard-working and versatile—able to bartend, serve, plate desserts, host and bus at the same time. Needless to say, I hired Karen as soon as she applied. She stayed for four years.

The second person to join our staff was Tony DeMelas, another artist and one of a dying breed of old-school professional waiters. Tony was elegant, gracious, mature, welcoming, able to handle a lot of customers, interested in wine and, of course, a prima donna. (Coincidentally, he had waited on my parents and me when we had lunch at Carolina's to celebrate my college graduation.) Carolina's was another La Terrasse offshoot and a significant Philadelphia neighborhood restaurant during the late 1980's and early 1990's. When I was in my early twenties and lived in Rittenhouse Square, my friends and I would always meet at Carolina's because it reminded us so much of La Terrasse, down to the curved bar, the food, the drink and the staff. Bill and Nancy Hoffman had worked at La Terrasse, and when they started Carolina's they brought a lot of the veteran La Terrasse staff with them.

It meant a lot to me that Tony had worked at Carolina's, because my experiences there had helped me formulate a vision for Fork. The bar scene was vibrant, and the restaurant was bistro style and priced as a neighborhood restaurant should be. Also in Tony's favor was the fact that a lot of people in Philadelphia knew Tony and what an incredible server he was. And he had a knack for recognizing regular customers, VIPs, press and restaurant owners. I knew that if

Tony DeMelas

Tony came on to our service team at Fork, other good servers would soon follow. Tony had a list of requirements—no lunches, no brunches, Friday and Saturday nights on the floor and he had to have time off whenever he had an art show. (I told you he was a prima donna!) I made a deal with him that was later used against me—not only by Tony, but also by other staff, who would always remind me that they didn't "do lunch."

As expected, once Tony was hired, he brought several people from Carolina's and La Terrasse (which had by then closed and reopened under new management), including Robert Caporusso, one of the best fine-dining bartenders in town, and Rebecca Kimball, an aspiring actress who later became manager. He also brought along Stephen Wood (S'woody), who became the most highly requested server at Fork; Vernon Sweet, who became dining-room manager; and Susan Johnston, my current loyal assistant.

With our key people in place, I wanted to minimize the potential for high drama on the service floor. So before the restaurant opened, we all agreed that staff members could not date one another. Roberto, who at the time was an extremely eligible bachelor, would joke about breaking this vow, but he never did. Despite our staff-wide agreement, however, Anne-Marie soon began dating Stephen, and the two were married shortly thereafter.

2

FORK GROWS UP

In 1997, the vision that Roberto, Anne-Marie and I shared was to open a neighborhood bistro. By 2000, we looked back and realized Fork had become much more than that; it had grown into a destination restaurant. Over the same period, the restaurant scene in Philadelphia had changed dramatically. When we opened in 1997, there was little competition in the neighborhood, so by definition Fork was a neighborhood restaurant. By 2000, however, Old City was known for its dining, nightlife and bars. Stephen Starr, one of Philadelphia's most prolific restaurateurs of the past twenty years, had begun to build his empire, with restaurants including The Continental, Buddakan and Tangerine, all of which opened within a three- to four-block radius in Old City. The rest of the city, too, was burgeoning with new restaurants with exciting food concepts, resulting in what observers have called Philadelphia's second Restaurant Renaissance. (The first was in the late 1970's.) One approach that was enabling more people to start restaurants was opening a BYOB (bring your own bottle) to avoid the expense of a liquor license.

Chef Dave Ballentine

Amid this growing competition, I felt the pressure to maintain and expand our customer base. In order for this to happen, it was critical for our customers to leave happy. We weren't the new kid on the block anymore, and most people love to try the latest new restaurant. To maintain our customer base and our reputation, we had to adapt more to our customers' needs, including making operational changes to accommodate them. Up until then, we had been open six days a week, closing only on Mondays. But some new restaurants in Old City were open on Mondays, so we felt we had no choice but to follow suit.

As a result, other changes had to be put in motion. We had to train others to manage the restaurant in order to be open seven days a week, and giving up control was an issue for Anne-Marie and me. Other differences also surfaced. Whereas Anne-Marie felt content with a small restaurant, one at which she could oversee all aspects of quality herself, I wanted Fork to keep growing and staying at the top of the restaurant scene in Philadelphia. Although we both loved Fork and wanted to offer guests a great experience, it became increasingly difficult for our differing goals to coexist. So Anne-Marie left Fork in December 2000, a little more than three years after we had opened. She and Stephen opened Picnic in 2001 in University City, a Philadelphia neighborhood that is home to the University of Pennsylvania and Drexel University, as well as to the White Dog Cafe and La Terrasse. Picnic offers fresh breakfast items, soups, salads and made-to-order sandwiches for take out, as well as catering.

Anne-Marie's departure resulted in a significant mood shift at Fork. Most times, Fork had seemed very much like a family. As hard as Anne-Marie was working, she was still the first one to set up Christmas stockings for the staff and stuff them with candy or to start dancing at the staff holiday party. Although the staff recognized that she and I had our differences, many felt as if their parents had gotten divorced. And when we brought on a new chef/partner, Dave Ballentine, staff members reacted as though he were the evil new boyfriend.

Dave and I had worked together at La Terrasse. He was one of the original chefs I had considered, and he was looking for a career change. His food was classic French, which was consistent with his training in the kitchens of restaurants such as The Frog, a major player in the first Philadelphia Restaurant Renaissance, and Odéon, another offshoot of La Terrasse. Since I loved the food and the service at all of the restaurants at which he had worked, Dave seemed like a natural to take Anne-Marie's place in Fork's kitchen.

transitioning:
the meal must go on!

While many guests did not notice the shift in chefs, the transition was challenging because we had to maintain and even improve the quality of our food despite many personnel changes. Cooks have often told me that when a chef leaves, the entire kitchen staff ultimately turns over, and in this case Fork was no exception. Under Anne-Marie, we'd had a great crew of line cooks. But even though Dave's personality was very low-key, friendly and nonthreatening, some staff decided to depart. Others stayed on and helped build the restaurant during this time of change.

Of course Dave's cooking style was of major interest to everyone involved. His style had evolved during the city's first Restaurant Renaissance, but a lot had changed since then. By the time Dave took the reins at Fork, the number of restaurants in Philadelphia had increased, and their style and presentation had grown more sophisticated and varied, with many new BYOBs and ethnic/international restaurants filling out the mix. In addition, Philadelphia diners were demanding more creativity, better presentation, better service and more value.

Up until this point, the menu at Fork had been rotating quickly. To maintain this concept required focus from the chef. Yet Dave was also raising a family—an equally important responsibility, if not more important. This made it difficult for him to focus intensely on creating an everchanging menu. Yet during his year-long tenure he made a major contribution to Fork by creating a management structure in the kitchen that allowed others to take over if the chef couldn't be there. He also brought some important dishes to our menu. One of Dave's signature dishes, which he brought to Fork from his days at Odéon, was a succulent crab cake, which was full of chunks of crab and contained little filler. Dave's recipe was simple, but the results were not the least bit ordinary.

The secret is to use jumbo lump crabmeat. Also, adding a little bit of mayonnaise prevents the cake from crumbling. Dave served his crab cakes with a creamy rémoulade.

sautéed crab cakes with serrano-pepper rémoulade

Serves 4 to 5 as a dinner first course or 2 to 3 as a lunch entrée

1 pound fresh jumbo lump crabmeat

⅓ cup Spanish onion, diced fine

¼ cup mayonnaise (see recipe in Fork Foundations or use prepared mayonnaise)

1 egg yolk

1 T Italian parsley, coarsely chopped

1 T lemon thyme

¼ cup fine breadcrumbs

salt, to taste

white pepper, to taste

cayenne pepper, to taste

3 T butter, plus more as needed

Carefully pick any shell fragments from crabmeat but leave meat as whole as possible. In a skillet over medium heat, melt 1 tablespoon butter. Add onions and sauté until translucent. Let onions cool. Place crabmeat in a bowl and add mayonnaise, onions, egg yolk and fresh herbs. Using a rubber spatula, carefully fold mixture to incorporate all ingredients. Add breadcrumbs, salt, pepper and a dash of cayenne pepper to taste. Fold mixture again. Divide mixture into 4-ounce portions and form into round cakes using cookie cutter. Melt remaining butter in a large sauté pan and sauté cakes over medium-high heat until they are crisp and golden brown on each side.

SERRANO-PEPPER RÉMOULADE

2 Serrano peppers, stems removed (and seeds and ribs removed for less intense heat), coarsely chopped

1 cup mayonnaise (make from recipe or use prepared)

2 T minced shallots or red onion

¼ cup cornichons (about 8), coarsely chopped

1 T lemon juice

2 T capers

½ tsp salt

Purée Serrano peppers with mayonnaise in a food processor or blender until smooth. Transfer to a small mixing bowl and fold in remaining ingredients.

While he was Fork's chef, Dave won *Philadelphia Magazine's* "2001 Dish of the Year." The winning dish, Pan-Seared Scallops with Brown Butter, Hazelnuts and White Truffle Oil, was unusual because white truffle oil was an uncommon ingredient on menus in Philadelphia at the time. White truffle oil's distinctive, earthy aroma is one that you either love or hate. It adds character to this simple scallop dish, which is delicious and easy to make. But be careful with the truffle oil; only a drop or two is needed. If you don't want to use truffle oil, the dish is still delicious.

Buying Fresh Scallops

At Fork we use dry scallops, which are caught, packed and shipped without preservatives. Most of the scallops available in supermarkets have been dipped in preservatives. These processed scallops do not work as well because they create excess liquid, which causes them to steam rather than pan sear. In addition, their flavor is vastly inferior. One way to distinguish between types is to look carefully at their color. Fresh, unprocessed scallops have an ivory or a light tan color. The preservatives in treated scallops cause them to look bright white, and they may even have a milky-white liquid surrounding them.

pan-seared scallops with brown butter, hazelnuts and white truffle oil aside roasted fingerling potatoes and asparagus

Serves 4 as a dinner main course

ROASTED FINGERLING POTATOES

1 pound fingerling potatoes, washed and sliced lengthwise

¼ cup olive oil

salt and freshly ground black pepper to taste

Preheat oven to 400°F. Toss fingerling potatoes with olive oil in a bowl. Season with salt and pepper to taste. Roast potatoes in a baking pan. Test with fork for tenderness. Remove from oven. Set aside.

ASPARAGUS

1 pound asparagus, washed, with tough ends removed

salt and freshly ground black pepper to taste

Blanch asparagus in boiling, salted water until it is bright green. Remove and plunge into an ice bath or rinse with cold water.

PAN-SEARED SCALLOPS

3 T extra-virgin olive oil

salt and freshly ground black pepper

12 to 16 jumbo sea scallops, or approximately 1½ pounds

9 T clarified butter (see recipe in Fork Foundations)

2 T lemon juice

1½ ounces hazelnuts, chopped coarsely and toasted

2 T chopped fresh parsley

1 or 2 drops white truffle oil (optional)

Heat a nonstick sauté pan until very hot. Add olive oil. Season scallops lightly with salt and pepper. When oil is hot, add scallops. Sauté first side approximately 2 minutes or until golden brown. Turn scallops in pan. After 1 minute, add butter and hazelnuts. When scallops are seared, remove from pan and place on a plate; keep warm.

Add lemon juice to butter and hazelnuts. When butter is browned, finish with chopped parsley. (Optional: Add a drop or two of white truffle oil to butter.) Toss potatoes and asparagus in brown butter until they are heated through. Place vegetables on plate. Position scallops over vegetables. Sprinkle with chopped parsley again to finish. Drizzle remaining brown butter over scallops.

This simple pasta recipe was one that Dave brought from La Terrasse to Odéon and then on to Fork. No added salt should be necessary, since the sauce has so much flavor from the olives and capers. This is the perfect lunch pasta or, if you are dining like Italians, a perfect precursor to your *secondi*.

pasta puttanesca

Serves 6 as an appetizer, 4 as an entrée

¼ cup extra-virgin olive oil

2 garlic cloves, mashed to a paste

½ T anchovy paste or chopped anchovies

¼ tsp red pepper flakes

⅓ cup dry white wine

1 T capers, chopped

¼ cup pitted black olives, chopped

1 pound fresh tomatoes, seeded, drained and diced

Juice of ½ a lemon (about 1 T)

1 cup fresh parsley leaves, chopped

1 pound penne pasta

shaved Parmigiano Reggiano, to taste

Heat olive oil in a large sauté pan over medium-high heat. Add garlic, anchovy paste and red pepper flakes and sauté briefly. Add wine and allow the mixture to simmer for about 2 minutes. Add capers, olives and diced tomatoes. Cook until the tomatoes just start to break down. Reduce heat to low.

Cook pasta al dente. Reserve ½ cup of the cooking water.

Add lemon juice and ½ cup reserved pasta water to sauce. Adjust seasoning with pepper. Add parsley and toss with hot pasta. Add shaved Parmigiano Reggiano and serve immediately. Pass extra cheese if desired.

Untitled, *Karen Gibson*

from our restaurant's kitchen:
a cookbook with a purpose

Roberto and I knew that maintaining the morale of our staff was important, but we found that it was particularly important during this time of change. Change is not easy for anyone to accept. So we needed a project that could involve everyone and create a stronger group identity.

We decided to go with one of our strengths. Over the past ten years, Fork's staff has had the notable characteristic of being committed to working together to help others. We have helped out at food drives and charitable events and given time to foster children's programs and the like. The art auction was a perfect example of one of our larger charitable projects. Because there were so many artists on staff and in Old City at the time, an art auction seemed like a natural way for us to raise money. SOS (Save Our Strength), a national antihunger organization and traditionally one of the restaurant industry's key causes, was the first beneficiary of our efforts. Naturally, the restaurant provided the food for the party. On auction were the creative contributions of staff and friends. There were about a dozen staff donations of paintings, jewelry, antiques and photos. We had some very accomplished artists on staff, so the quality was impressive. Other staff members also made donations, offering time for bartending lessons, picnics, catered dinners and even a wine tasting. All in all, we auctioned almost three dozen items and services and raised seven thousand dollars.

After the first auction, some members of the staff—particularly Gigi Tevlin-Moffat, one of our more vocal servers—felt that our efforts should be focused more locally so that our donation would help people nearby. One suggestion was that we create some sort of a scholarship for an inner-city student. But we didn't know how to set up a scholarship or how to work with the school district to identify possible scholarship recipients.

Pear, *Anthony DeMelas*

Oh Brother, *Paul Rodriguez*

Coincidentally, our long-time customer Howard Goldstein taught at the Jules E. Mastbaum Vocational Arts High School within the School District of Philadelphia. When we consulted Howard, he just assumed we were putting together a culinary scholarship and mentioned that Mastbaum has an excellent culinary-arts program.

We all liked the idea of a culinary scholarship and of working with Howard's school, but Gigi found that it would be too complicated for us to donate money to students through the school district. Instead, we identified another organization, Careers in Culinary Arts Program (C-CAP), through which we could award scholarships. C-CAP was already working with the School District of Philadelphia to provide educational opportunities for inner-city youth through scholarships, mentoring and training. C-CAP allowed us to donate the monies raised by our art auctions and to direct it to several Philadelphia students per year.

But after several auctions, their yield declined. To keep the scholarship going, we decided to write and publish a cookbook. The book, which came out in late 2001 and is called *From Our Restaurant's Kitchen,* included recipes for some of our signature dishes but offered an equal number of recipes donated by our staff, along with visual images of art works made by staff members.

Our staff's effort was commendable. Even former employees wanted to participate in the book. Twenty-five hundred books later, the book was sold out and we had raised sixteen-thousand dollars for our scholarship fund, which went to assist students at prestigious hospitality programs such as the Culinary Institute of America, Johnson and Wales, the Swiss Hospitality Institute, the Restaurant School and the Art Institute of Philadelphia.

When we were writing the book, our current chef, Thien Ngo, was still a line cook, but he had already begun developing menu items to help Dave. His gazpacho has been a longstanding Fork favorite. He insists that gazpacho should be an improvisation and makes it with whatever is ripe and available, keeping in mind the aim of creating an appealing balance of flavors. The recipe that follows is a tropical-fruit gazpacho that takes advantage of summer fruits and is perfect in the hot weather.

spicy tropical-fruit gazpacho with avocado

Serves 6

3 cups tomato juice

1 mango, peeled and cut into small chunks

5 medium tomatoes, chopped and seeded

3 garlic cloves, minced and smashed into a paste with 1 tsp coarse salt

½ cup cucumber, diced into small pieces

½ cup pineapple, diced into small pieces

½ cup red onion, chopped fine

¼ cup lime juice

1 cup fresh cilantro, chopped

1 cup fresh parsley, chopped

1 tsp cumin

1 jalapeño pepper, cored and seeded, minced fine

¼ cup lime juice

2 ripe avocados, peeled and pitted right before serving

In a blender, purée 2 cups tomato juice with all but ¼ cup mango chunks. Transfer purée to a large bowl and add remaining ingredients. Season with salt and pepper to taste. Cover and chill for several hours to allow the flavors to come together.

Garnish with avocado wedges.

A Sunday Drive, *Paul Rodriguez*

Civet is a traditional French stew made from game (such as wild rabbit, wild boar or venison), pearl onions and bacon. The braising liquid is typically made from red wine thickened with some of the animal's blood. Even if you omit the blood, the civet should have a gamey flavor.

Thien's recipe for duck civet (pronounced *see* VAY) was one of the more challenging recipes in the book. However, it is worth the effort. Whenever Thien makes duck civet, I am reminded of my mom's cooking. And whenever my mom eats it, she says, "This is just like Chinese cooking," even though Thien considers it a distinctly French recipe. The recipe could be modified for use with any sort of game, such as rabbit or pheasant.

thien's duck civet

Serves 4 as a dinner main course

4 medium carrots, diced fine

2 stalks celery, diced fine

1 medium onion, peeled and
   diced fine

1 small leek, white parts only,
   diced fine

3 T unsalted butter

1 whole duck or 2 duck legs and
   2 duck breasts

1½ cups merlot

1½ cups chicken stock

2 cups port, divided

2 ounces cognac

3 bay leaves

½ cup green olives, pitted
   and chopped

1 cup pearl onions, blanched

1 bunch baby carrots, blanched

¼ cup clarified butter (see recipe
   in Fork Foundations)

salt and freshly ground black pepper
   to taste

1 pound pappardelle

Preheat grill. Preheat oven to 350°F. Heat butter in a medium saucepan over high heat. Add carrots, celery, onion and leeks and cook until tender. Season with salt and pepper and set aside.

Season duck with salt and pepper. Place duck on hot grill. Fat drippings will cause some flare-ups. Once duck is blackened on about half of its skin, turn and repeat on other side. Remove from flame and allow to cool enough so you can separate the duck into two legs and two breasts, if working with whole duck.

Preheat oven to 350°F. Place duck pieces in a roasting pan with merlot, chicken stock and 1 cup port. Cover completely with sautéed carrot, celery and onion mixture and season with salt and pepper. Pour cognac over duck evenly. Using bay leaves as "matches," light leaves and ignite duck. After alcohol has burned off, place pan in oven and roast, uncovered, for 1½ hours.

Remove duck from roasting pan and set aside. Add remaining 1 cup port and continue cooking sauce on stovetop until it is reduced and thickened. Strain sauce through chinois or strainer. Stir olives into sauce.

In a hot skillet, heat clarified butter. Over high heat, place duck skin-side down and sear both sides until golden brown. Remove duck.

Boil salted water and cook pappardelle.

Sauté pearl onions and baby carrots in a small amount of sauce until lightly caramelized. Melt 1 tablespoon of butter into vegetables to finish.

To Serve: Toss freshly cooked pappardelle with sauce in a large bowl. Place duck, pearl onions and baby carrots over pasta. Ladle extra sauce onto plates as desired.

As I think about the six hundred or so staff people who have passed through Fork over the years, a few in particular stand out in my mind. Rachel Rogala is one of those people. Previously a managing editor for the *Philadelphia Weekly*, Rachel was our office manager for two years and helped me maintain my sanity. After her Fork career, she became a freelancer for the local papers and then a grant writer for Children's Hospital of Philadelphia. This recipe appeared first in the *Philadelphia Daily News*, where she had a column called "Sandwich Board." It's a great summer dessert for the kid in you.

chocolate-chip-cookie sandwich with coffee gelato and chocolate sauce

Serves 8

CHOCOLATE-CHIP COOKIE

½ pound unsalted butter, softened

1½ cups light brown sugar

2 cups unbleached flour

2 tsp baking soda

2 tsp salt

½ tsp vanilla extract

1 cup chocolate chips

Preheat oven to 350°F. Thoroughly grease a jelly-roll pan (or pans, depending on their size) with butter. In a mixer, cream butter and brown sugar until they turn pale in color. In a separate bowl, sift together flour, baking soda and salt. Fold sifted ingredients into creamed mixture. Stir in vanilla. Add chocolate chips. Turn mixture onto pan(s) and spread evenly. Bake for 25 minutes. When cool, cut into squares measuring approximately 5 by 5 inches, then cut each into triangles.

COFFEE GELATO

2½ cups milk

1½ cups heavy cream

3 T cornstarch

1 cup sugar

1 tsp vanilla extract

5 T instant coffee

Heat heavy cream and 1½ cups of the milk on stovetop to a boil, then reduce to a simmer. In a bowl, whisk together remaining milk, cornstarch, sugar and vanilla. Combine two mixtures by slowly pouring second into simmering milk, stirring constantly until thickened. Remove from heat. Cover and refrigerate overnight or until thoroughly chilled. Add coffee and mix in, then freeze in an ice-cream maker according to the manufacturer's instructions. Once gelato is frozen, turn onto a sheet or jelly-roll pan and spread evenly. Cover lightly and freeze until hard.

CHOCOLATE SAUCE

4 ounces high-quality semisweet chocolate

1 pint heavy cream

In a double boiler or a metal bowl placed securely over boiling water, melt chocolate. Add heavy cream and stir well.

To assemble: With a clean knife or spatula and using a cookie as a template, cut gelato into triangles. Place ice cream between two cookies. Top with chocolate sauce and serve.

Mojo typically refers to a hot sauce that originated in the Canary Islands and has since emigrated to Cuba, Venezuela, the Caribbean and beyond. A basic mojo consists of olive oil, large amounts of garlic, paprika or chili powder and cumin. Flavorings such as vinegar or the juice of lemons, oranges and limes may be added, along with tomatoes or avocado. In Cuban cooking, mojo refers to any sauce made with garlic, olive oil and citrus juice.

Among the many staff recipes in our fundraising cookbook, one of the most interesting was Gail Lazio's Venezuelan Mojo. Perhaps I found it particularly interesting because Venezuelan cuisine is not yet widely known in Philadelphia. This recipe was inspired by her childhood in Venezuela. Gail is an interior designer who moonlighted as a host at Fork. Though she had no previous restaurant experience, she was one of our most friendly and well-liked hosts.

venezuelan mojo

Makes 2 cups

2 ripe avocados

⅓ cup chopped onion

1 red bell pepper, chopped

1 green bell pepper, chopped

4 aji dulce or Italian sweet peppers,
    2 red and 2 green, chopped

4 garlic cloves, minced

¾ cup cilantro leaves, chopped

⅓ cup vegetable oil

4 T white vinegar

juice from ½ lemon

optional: jalapeño pepper, diced fine,
    to taste

Cut avocados in half. Remove pits and scoop flesh from shells. Mash with a fork in a bowl. Add remaining ingredients and mix until lumpy. Chill for 3 to 4 hours. Serve over grilled meats, chicken or seafood.

Another unusual recipe inspired by a family's home cooking was server
Eun Kim's Korean-style marinade. Though she admits that it is not a
traditional marinade, she uses this dish when she wishes to introduce
Korean flavors to friends who have never tried Korean food. Eun was
a server at Fork for a few years before she went on to attend the Culinary
Institute of America.

chicken skewers with
spicy korean marinade

Serves 10 to 12 as an hors d'oeuvre or 4 to 6 as a lunch entrée

SPICY KOREAN MARINADE

4 cloves garlic, crushed

juice of 2 limes

2 T sesame oil

2 jalapeño peppers, sliced thin

1 T fish sauce

1 T soy sauce

2 T hot red pepper paste (can be
found in most Asian markets;
if you cannot find it, mix 2 T chili
powder into 1 T tomato paste—
not the same flavor, but gets the
job done)

2 T sugar

1 T sea salt

3 scallions, chopped

¼ cup orange juice

Mix all ingredients in bowl. Set aside.

CHICKEN SKEWERS

1½ to 2 pounds chicken breast

long wood skewers

Slice chicken breasts into long strips,
½ inch wide. Toss with marinade
and let sit in refrigerator for at least
2 hours. Meanwhile, soak skewers
in water so they won't burn when
you put them on the grill. After
chicken has marinated, place strips
lengthwise onto skewers and grill on
medium-high heat for approximately
5 minutes on each side, or until
cooked through. The number of
skewers depends on the amount of
chicken used. This recipe is a great
party hors d'oeuvre, or you could
serve over rice as an entrée.

a new chef, a new direction

If there is one thing I've learned over the years, it's that no one is indispensable. Yet I have to keep reminding myself that this is the case. Whenever a key person announces his or her departure, or in some cases just stops showing up, I think to myself, "This is it. How could so and so leave me? I'll never be able to do it without ____." Somehow, however, someone capable ends up on my doorstep. At times I have had to put out ads, to interview, to network and contact schools; at other times, as was the case with our current chef, serendipity takes over.

Thien Ngo (pronounced *TEE' yen No*) walked in one day during Dave's tenure. Dave's sous chef, Alicia Agnolotti, had worked with Thien at the nuevo-Latino restaurant ¡Pasion!, which was co-owned by Guillermo Pernot, an ex-La Terrasser. Although most of our shifts were full, Alicia said that Thien was good and that we should try to hire him somehow. But during my initial meeting with him, I had my doubts. Thien is small in stature, only five feet two inches tall. I thought to myself, "Will this guy be able to work on such a fast-paced line?" And when Dave asked for his résumé, Thien said that he didn't have one. (Thien loves to tell this to every new kitchen employee. He had to prove himself by his ability, not with a piece of paper.) Nevertheless, knowing that one day we could be fully staffed and the next day lacking, we tried to figure out how to accommodate Thien in the kitchen. All we could come up with was one shift, Friday lunch. But Thien accepted the job, even though we offered only eleven dollars an hour. (Thien also loves to tell this story to aspiring young cooks, because it proves that any talented line cook has the potential to become chef!)

It didn't take long for Thien to stretch his muscles and show off his comprehensive cooking experience. Nor did it take him long to share his story with us. Over the next few weeks I learned that Thien had been born in Vietnam and had worked all over the world, including in Switzerland, France, Japan and New Orleans. He had been executive sous chef at Avenue B, a restaurant owned by the well-known Philadelphia restaurateur Neil Stein, which had been located across from Philadelphia's brand new Kimmel Center. The restaurant was ahead of its time; it opened before the construction of the new concert hall was complete, and sadly its potentially beautiful outdoor café and bar did not survive.

At first I didn't know what to think about Thien. When he arrived, our cooks wore Fork T-shirts, with the exception of Dave. Anne-Marie had hated the traditional chef's jacket as a daily work uniform and embraced the T-shirt substitute. But both Thien and Dave insisted that they would not wear Fork T-shirts in the kitchen. It went against their professional opinion of themselves. Instead, they wore chef's jackets, and Thien completed the picture with a black skullcap. Many people, including our customers and our kitchen staff, were fascinated by his hat. Eventually, the entire kitchen staff donned skullcaps!

Thien has also distinguished himself by refusing to call me by my first name. Instead, he calls me "Ma'am." When I told him to please call me Ellen, he asked why I didn't want him to call me the more dignified title he preferred. By doing so, he said, he is showing respect for me in front of the kitchen staff. I had nothing to say. But after seven years on the job he still calls me "Ma'am," though sometimes he slips and calls me "Mom."

Chef Thien Ngo

Not long after his arrival, I asked Thien if he would work at Fork full time, and several weeks later he announced that he wanted to join us. Knowing that he was not a resource to be wasted, I quickly organized a meeting with Roberto, Dave and Thien to discuss Thien's role in the kitchen. But figuring out his role was not easy. Even though Thien offered to help in whatever ways Dave wished, talented people are not the easiest people to work with, and Thien was no exception. He was always challenging the equilibrium. During his first shift on the line at night, for instance, he challenged one of the veteran waitstaff. Normally, it is understood that an entrée is put up (ready to go to the table) approximately ten minutes after it is fired (placed with the kitchen by the waitperson). But in this case, Thien put up the order in two minutes. Then he told the waitperson, "I can see you're not ready, so why did you fire it? Because you think I can't make it fast enough?" To make matters worse, he refused to make the item again so that it would be ready when the customer was ready to enjoy it. The server was infuriated. I tried to explain to Thien that the front-of-house staff expected items to be ready ten minutes after they were fired, but Thien replied that he responds to the ticket when it's fired and that it's not his job to keep track of how much time has passed. Point taken.

Despite his abrasiveness, Roberto and I knew that Thien could be a tremendous asset. But we didn't want to step on Dave's toes. As we worked to define Thien's role, we considered the fact that Dave was not able to spend enough time at the restaurant to focus on menu changes because of family obligations. I suggested that perhaps Thien could relieve Dave of some of the menu-development responsibilities, but Dave didn't want to relinquish that work. Instead, he thought it would be most helpful to have Thien make desserts. So Thien became the pastry chef. Rather than being upset about being assigned to an area in which he had no real experience, Thien just shrugged his shoulders and started arriving at 5 A.M.

This presented us with an interesting situation. Over the past ten years I have figured out that chefs can make "chef" desserts but do not usually make good pastry chefs. Thien was no exception. His first dessert was a four-cheese cheesecake made from cream cheese, brie, goat cheese and Roquefort. I liked the idea of something off the wall, but when I tasted it, I knew that it would not be the cheesecake our diners would expect. In fact, some people, including our waitstaff, were even a bit disgusted by it. His White-Chocolate Carrot Cake, on the other hand, was a hit. Its creamy, cheesecake-like texture always leaves you wanting another bite.

white-chocolate carrot cake with macadamia-nut topping

Makes one 9-inch round cake

CRUST

2 cups graham-cracker crumbs

6 T butter, melted

⅓ cup sugar

pinch of salt

Preheat oven to 350°F. Stir together graham-cracker crumbs, melted butter and sugar. Spread and pack mixture on bottom of a 9-inch spring-form pan and bake for 15 to 20 minutes, until just browned around the edges. Set aside and let cool completely.

Turn the oven to 375°F.

WHITE-CHOCOLATE CARROT CAKE

½ pound carrots, peeled and cut into chunks

8 ounces cream cheese, room temperature

1½ cups sugar

¼ tsp fine salt

4 ounces macadamia nuts, toasted

¼ tsp fresh-ground nutmeg

1½ tsp vanilla extract

5 eggs

¾ cup white chocolate chips or pieces, chopped

¼ cup plus 2 T flour

Put carrot chunks in a pot, cover with water and bring to a boil. Cook until fork tender. Strain and let cool in colander so they will dry off.

Process toasted nuts with sugar and salt in a food processor until they are sandy. Set aside in a bowl. Transfer carrots to food processor and purée.

Beat cream cheese in a stand mixer fitted with paddle attachment until soft and light. Add puréed carrots and beat again to combine with cream cheese thoroughly. Add nut mixture, nutmeg and vanilla and continue mixing to combine. Beat eggs separately until foamy, then slowly pour into carrot mixture with machine on low speed. Add chopped chocolate and flour; mix just until incorporated.

Pour batter over crust in spring-form pan. Bake at 375°F for 45 minutes. Cover pan with foil and continue baking an additional 20 minutes. Remove from oven. Sides will be set and center may be a bit wobbly. Allow to cool completely in pan.

MACADAMIA-NUT TOPPING

8 ounces cream cheese, room temperature

2 cups sifted confectioner's sugar

12 ounces white chocolate

⅔ cup heavy cream

½ cup toasted macadamia nuts, chopped

Beat cream cheese and sugar together until they are light and fluffy. Combine white chocolate and cream in a medium saucepan and melt together over medium-low heat, stirring often. When chocolate has melted into cream, set aside to cool slightly. With mixer running, pour melted-chocolate mixture into cream-cheese mixture. Beat together until completely incorporated. Cover and let set while cake cools.

Pour frosting over cooled cake in pan and sprinkle with macadamia nuts. Cover and refrigerate at least one hour or until ready to serve. Remove from spring-form pan to cut and serve.

fork turns five

Ever since I was a child, early fall has been my favorite time of year. When I was younger it signaled the beginning of a new cycle; usually that meant starting school and meeting new friends. Even now, fall is my favorite season. After a hot summer, it is always refreshing to see our regular customers reappear. Fall also marks the beginning of the new theater and arts calendars, so our business is usually brisk. Fall is definitely Fork's season: the coziness of the restaurant, the warmth of the lampshades and the sights and sounds of the open kitchen are comforting as the weather starts to chill. And since Fork opened in mid-October 1997, we celebrate its anniversary in the fall.

In terms of restaurant anniversary dates, every year matters for the first three years, because the survival of a restaurant is considered uncertain until that point. The next milestone to be noted is the fifth year. Once you've passed five years, you've established yourself, and nothing counts until your tenth year, by which time you're an institution! Our fifth anniversary came during another time of transition, as Dave had left the restaurant at the beginning of 2002 and Thien had just taken the reins in the kitchen. We celebrated our fifth anniversary in October 2002 with a special press dinner to thank the local food-writing community for having supported us for so long. Thien put a great deal of effort into the menu, and some of the dishes served became regular features of Thien's Fork repertoire.

One of those recipes was a beet salad. Over the years, Thien has created numerous salads with beets. They all involve some sort of distinctive fruit, such as kiwi, melon, peaches, passion fruit, mango, persimmon, papaya or Asian pear, with a salad dressing that helps to balance out the flavors. Sometimes he throws in avocado or cheese. This recipe was one of his first creations with beets.

Toasting nuts brings out their natural flavors and intensifies their crunch. Nuts can be toasted in a skillet over medium-high heat or in a moderately hot oven (about 300°F) on a sheet pan for 5 to 10 minutes. Shake pan occasionally and be careful not to let nuts burn. This can happen very quickly once they have toasted. Nuts are done as soon as you can smell their toasted aroma.

Roasting beets is easy. Just follow these instructions.

Preheat oven to 350°F.
Wash beets and cut off their tops. Place beets in roasting pan and cover with water. Cover pan with foil and roast in oven for about 1 hour or until beets are fork tender. Allow them to cool in liquid. When cool, remove their peels, using your fingers or a paring knife. Beets can be prepared up to 2 days in advance and stored in the refrigerator.

roasted beets, kiwi and baby greens with green-peppercorn vinaigrette

Serves 4 as a dinner appetizer or 2 as a lunch entrée

GREEN-PEPPERCORN VINAIGRETTE

1 T green peppercorns in brine, drained

⅓ cup white-wine or white-balsamic vinegar

1 shallot, minced

1 clove garlic, minced

1 T plus 1 tsp honey

1 tsp salt

freshly ground black pepper

⅔ cup olive oil

Combine peppercorns, vinegar, shallot, garlic, honey, salt and pepper in a food processor and purée mixture. With processor running, add olive oil in a slow, steady stream, allowing mixture to emulsify. Transfer to a container and set aside. (Can be made up to a week in advance and stored in refrigerator.)

ROASTED BEETS, KIWI AND BABY GREENS

4 medium red beets, roasted or cut into quarters (or eighths if beets are very large)

4 ripe kiwis, peeled, cut in quarters

baby arugula or other baby greens

In a bowl, mix beets and kiwis with approximately ¼ cup of vinaigrette. Place equal parts of beets and kiwi on four chilled plates. Arrange salad on plate. Drizzle dressing around plate.

White balsamic vinegar is used frequently at Fork. Most of us are accustomed to red balsamic vinegar, but authentic Italian balsamic vinegar (*aceto balsamico tradizionale*) is made with white wine that has been cooked down to a thick, syrupy consistency and then fermented and aged in special wooden casks for a minimum of twelve years. Aged balsamic doesn't need to be mixed with other ingredients because the rich, sweet vinegar is so pure and smooth that it stands on its own. If it is not labeled aceto balsamico tradizionale, chances are that it was made from red wine and fortified with concentrated grape juice or even caramelized sugar. White balsamic vinegar is milder and less sweet than traditional balsamic vinegar and is ideal for use in cooking, deglazing and making vinaigrettes.

Many Philadelphians first sampled octopus because of the popular Greek seafood restaurant Dmitri's, which has been serving up marinated grilled octopus for at least fifteen years. My routine at Dmitri's is to arrive and get on the waiting list, have a drink at a bar across the street called the New Wave Cafe, then bring my favorite bottle of rosé to Dmitri's and enjoy a few of their small plates, including octopus, their featured dish. To me, Dmitri's is a phenomenon. Its food is consistent and always tasty, and its culture remains the same, no matter who is working there. Dmitri's has opened up other outposts, but in my humble opinion the one at Third and Catherine Streets is the best! The octopus, made by a crew of cooks from Laos, is perfectly seasoned and always tender.

Fork's octopus is made by a Vietnamese chef who uses baby octopus. Baby octopus has to be very carefully cooked, as otherwise it quickly becomes tough or rubbery. If you don't have access to baby octopus or if you are squeamish about it, substitute calamari.

grilled baby octopus aside cucumber and radish with lime-scallion vinaigrette

Serves 4 as a dinner appetizer or 2 as a lunch entrée

LIME-SCALLION VINAIGRETTE

zest of 2 limes

⅓ cup freshly squeezed lime juice (from about 4 limes)

1 bunch scallions, cleaned and cut into 1-inch pieces

1 garlic clove, roughly chopped

1 small shallot, roughly chopped (about 1 T)

1 T plus 1 tsp honey

1 tsp salt

freshly ground black pepper

⅔ cup olive oil

Combine zest, juice, scallions, garlic, shallot, honey, salt and pepper in a blender or food processor and purée. With processor running, add olive oil in a slow, steady stream, allowing mixture to emulsify. Transfer to a container and set aside.

GRILLED BABY OCTOPUS

16 to 24 baby octopus, thawed

Preheat grill. In a large bowl, toss octopus with half of the vinaigrette.

Grill octopus for a few minutes, until it is translucent. Remove from heat. Season with salt and pepper to taste.

1 cucumber, seeded and cut on a bias

8 radishes, quartered

baby greens

Toss cucumber and radishes in half of the remaining vinaigrette. Place equal parts on chilled plates. Arrange equal parts of octopus on plates. Drizzle remaining vinaigrette on top. Garnish with baby greens.

The interns (left to right: Ellen, Stephanie Park, Anna McGorman, Meredith Swinney, Rachel Berger, Sous Chef Christina McKeough)

The quince is a hard, yellow fruit that is similar in appearance and texture to apples and pears. Too hard and sour to eat raw, quinces are used to make jam or jelly. They can also be peeled and then roasted, baked or stewed. The fruit turns reddish-orange during cooking. Do not eat the seeds, as they are poisonous.

When Thien worked in Paris, he moved up the ranks in the cooking hierarchy to achieve the title Cuisinier de la Premiere Classe (first-class cook). Part of his training involved making different types of charcuterie, which he did extremely well. He could make pâté, sausage or terrines from anything, including duck, rabbit, venison, foie gras, monkfish liver or tofu. What follows is one of his most tasty pâtés. Served with the authentic combination of grainy mustard, toast points and cornichons, along with Thien's own quince compote, it makes a memorable appetizer or lunch.

country pâté with quince compote, grainy mustard, cornichons and toast points

Serves 8 as a dinner appetizer or lunch entrée

QUINCE COMPOTE

6 quince, peeled and cored

1 cup lemon juice

1 cup sugar

Combine all ingredients in a medium saucepan over medium heat. Stir regularly until mixture caramelizes, about 20 to 30 minutes. Remove from heat and let cool.

COUNTRY PÂTÉ

¾ pound duck confit, pureéd (see recipe for duck confit on page 97)

¼ pound chicken livers, deveined

1 head of shallot, with each shallot cut into quarters

peeled cloves of 1 head of garlic

3 T butter

¼ pound ground pork or lamb

3 T honey

2 tsp salt

¼ cup cognac

¼ cup pistachios, toasted

2 T green peppercorns

2 T truffle peelings

1 T truffle oil

Preheat oven to 350°F. Combine chicken livers, shallot, garlic and butter in a small baking dish. Bake in oven about 5 minutes. Remove livers and set aside. Cover dish with foil and return garlic and shallots to oven for an additional 30 minutes.

Remove from oven when tender and allow to cool slightly. Transfer to food processor with all juices in dish, plus livers, and purée to a paste.

In a stand mixer fitted with hook attachment, combine pureéd chicken livers, garlic and shallot with the pureéd duck confit. Add honey, salt, cognac, truffle peelings, oil, ground pork or lamb, and peppercorns. Mix until well combined. Add pistachios and mix briefly to incorporate.

Lay a sheet of plastic wrap on table. Top with pâté and roll to form a log about 12 inches long and 3 inches thick. Wrap in foil and transfer to a baking sheet. Roast 45 minutes. Remove from oven; allow to cool completely. Refrigerate until ready to serve. Slice pâté through foil and plastic wrap into pieces about ½ inch thick (remove foil and wrap before serving). Serve with grainy mustard, cornichons, toast points and quince compote.

This pâté keeps well. Keep unused portion in aluminum foil. Wrap end with plastic wrap. Just trim off the end before serving again.

Quail is a delicate bird with a mildly gamey flavor. In the fall, Thien always adds quail to Fork's menu. For me his quail dishes make the perfect light and somewhat festive dinner. This one is very simple to make.

pan-roasted quail with roasted pears, frisée and pistachios

Serves 4 as a dinner appetizer or a light dinner/lunch

MARINADE AND QUAIL

1½ cups extra-virgin olive oil

3 cloves garlic, peeled, smashed

1 T fresh rosemary, chopped

1 T fresh thyme, chopped

2 T shallots, chopped fine

4 quails, chest bone removed

Combine all ingredients in a large bowl. Marinate quail for 2 hours.

ROASTED PEARS

4 Seckel or Bosc pears

¼ cup lemon juice

¼ cup honey

2 T cold butter, cut into small pieces

salt and freshly ground black pepper

Preheat oven to 350°F. Mix pears with lemon juice and honey in a small baking dish. Sprinkle butter pieces across pears. Bake until a toothpick can be inserted (45 minutes for Seckel pears, 1 hour 20 minutes for Bosc pears). Remove from heat; allow to cool. Seckel pears can be served whole. Bosc pears can be cut in half and cored.

PAN-ROASTED QUAIL

Preheat oven to 400°F. Remove quail from marinade and season with salt and pepper. Heat 1 tablespoon olive oil in a large sauté pan over high heat. Sear chests of quail until they are golden brown. Turn. Squeeze ½ teaspoon honey over each quail. Transfer to oven in same pan and roast for 12 minutes.

FRISÉE AND PISTACHIO SALAD

1 head frisée, cleaned

½ cup pistachios, toasted

½ cup extra-virgin olive oil

2 T lemon juice

salt and freshly ground black pepper

In a small bowl, whisk together olive oil and lemon juice. Season with salt and pepper. Place a small bed of frisée on each plate.

To assemble plates, gently remove quail from pan and position on each plate. Add a pear and a drizzle of quail jus. Sprinkle with pistachios. Serve immediately.

Boniato is sometimes called a white sweet potato. It could be considered a cross between a regular baking potato and a sweet potato and can be cooked in the same manner. Boniato is fluffier, drier and less sweet than yellow or orange sweet potatoes and has a pinkish skin. Store boniato at room temperature, not in the refrigerator. Once it has been peeled, boniato should be used immediately or immersed in cold water to avoid discoloration. When boiling boniato, submerge it in water completely to avoid blotching.

Braised meat always reminds me of my mother's cooking. She made braised spare ribs, oxtails, chicken feet, pork shoulder and more. I loved the tenderness of the meat, and the braising liquid was my favorite part. I would create a simple meal by pouring some of the braising liquid over a plate of white rice. The recipe for braised lamb shank also produces a tender meat combined with an equally delicious sauce. The first time I had a lamb shank, I had to laugh. I felt as though I were Fred Flintstone, eating a big bone. The hind leg is bigger; the fore leg is smaller and leaner. I prefer the hind leg because the fat in it adds more flavor to the sauce, but you can choose whichever you prefer for this recipe.

braised lamb shank in port-wine orange jus with creamy mashed boniato and sautéed swiss chard

Serves 4 as a dinner main dish

BRAISED LAMB SHANK

4 shanks

3 T olive oil

flour

salt and freshly ground black pepper

1 carrot, coarsely chopped

1 stalk celery, coarsely chopped

1 white onion, coarsely chopped

2 cloves garlic, whole

2 T tomato paste

1 cup port

2 cups orange juice

3 cups meat or chicken stock (see recipe in Fork Foundations or use store-bought)

2 star anise, whole

6 whole cloves

1 bunch fresh parsley

1 bunch fresh thyme

1 bunch fresh rosemary

cheesecloth and butcher's string

Preheat oven to 350°F. Season shanks with salt and pepper. Dust in flour. In a large roasting pan on stove, heat oil over high heat. Add shanks and sear until they are browned on all sides. Remove shanks from pan and set aside.

In same roasting pan, add onions and garlic. Sauté until caramelized. Add carrots and celery and sauté 5 minutes. Add tomato paste. Deglaze pan with port wine.

Return shanks to pan. Add orange juice and stock. Place star anise, clove, parsley, thyme and rosemary in a cheesecloth, tie mixture together with butcher's string and add it to liquid in pan. Cover pan with aluminum foil. Braise in oven for 2½ hours, until meat begins to fall off bones. While shanks are cooking, prepare boniato.

Remove from heat and let shanks cool. Remove shanks from braising liquid. Skim fat off (it should have floated to the top). Save liquid and strain it through chinois. Reduce liquid in a small saucepan over medium heat until thickened, about 20 minutes.

CREAMY MASHED BONIATO

2½ pounds boniato, peeled and cut into 1-inch cubes

1 cup milk or cream, warmed

2 T cold butter, cut into small pieces

1 tsp Kosher salt, or more to taste

freshly ground black pepper

Put boniato cubes in a large pot and fill with water, covering by about 2 inches. Bring water to a boil, reduce to simmer and cook for 10 to 15 minutes, or until boniato is fork tender. Drain boniato and return it to pot. Add butter and warm milk and mix with an electric mixer to consistency of mashed potatoes. Season with salt and pepper to taste.

SAUTÉED SWISS CHARD

2 cups Swiss chard, cleaned

1 clove garlic, minced

1 T olive oil

salt and freshly ground black pepper to taste

Heat oil in pan. When hot, add garlic. Reduce heat if necessary. Do not burn garlic. Add Swiss chard and cook until wilted. Season with salt and pepper.

To assemble dish, place one serving each of mashed boniato and sautéed greens into individual pasta dishes. Gently place a lamb shank into each bowl. Pour braising liquid over shank to finish. Serve immediately.

This simple, easy-to-make dessert is a great ending to a big meal.
You can also use these poached pears on a salad or place them aside
duck confit or pâté.

port-poached bosc pears with ginger

Serves 4

one 750-ml bottle (or about 3 cups) port

1 cup sugar

three 1-inch pieces of ginger, peeled

4 Bosc pears, peeled, with stem remaining

Combine port and sugar in a medium pot over high heat. Stir until sugar dissolves. Add pears and ginger and bring liquid to a boil over high heat. Reduce heat to medium-low and simmer for 30 to 40 minutes, until pears are tender. Remove from heat.

Leaving pears in poaching liquid, allow them to cool before refrigerating. When ready to serve, place a pear in each chilled bowl. Serve aside sorbet or gelato.

kids can eat at fork, too

Fork has always been child- and baby-friendly. I don't mean to imply that we have an extensive children's menu, but just that we have never frowned upon anyone who brings their kids, whether they are infants or teens. Maybe we are child-friendly because the two people running Fork at the start were women in their thirties whose biological clocks were ticking, or possibly it's because being a restaurant owner is like parenting, so a natural simpatico exists. While our older customers may not always be able to order whatever they want, children always can. Even since Anne-Marie left the restaurant, children have always been treated as VIPs. And at any meal that has included the children of my friends or family, Thien always makes something special. If a child has a special request, whatever it might be, he will satisfy it with pleasure.

Usually, children are drawn to Thien. They remember his name from one visit to the next and love to go see him in his office. One child of special note at Fork is Harrison, the son of Meg Rodgers, the interior designer who helped create Fork, and her husband, James Timberlake. Meg has always been integral to our business. The first time I met her, I knew that she had to be the one to convert our vacant shell into a beautiful dining room. Before her work on Fork, she had designed some of the most beautiful dining rooms in Philadelphia. The most well known of these was the original Striped Bass owned by Neil Stein, which was one of Philadelphia's most elegant dining establishments. Stein's restaurant was housed in a gorgeous, ornate space at the corner of Fifteenth and Walnut Streets, the former offices of an investment house called Butcher and Singer. (The restaurant still exists at the same site and was redesigned by its new owners.)

Thien, Veronica and Harrison

Meg accepted the job, and midway through the construction of Fork she announced that she and James were going to have a baby. Harrison was born in January 1998. From the beginning, whether he was in the womb or out, Harrison was with his mother on job sites, at the restaurant or at her office. Wherever Meg went, so did Harrison. Naturally, because he and his parents frequented the restaurant often, Harrison became a part of the Fork family. The Timberlake-Rodgers family was so in sync with Fork that when Fork decided to expand in 2004, so did their family. Their daughter, Veronica, was adopted from China in February 2004 and is now another member of the Fork family.

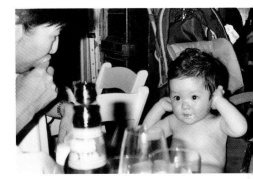

One can say of any child that he or she grows over the years, but Harrison is not a typical child. James is at least six feet two inches tall, and Harrison inherited his dad's height. At age four, he looked like a six year old; by age nine, he was almost as tall as me (I'm five feet four inches tall). Aside from heredity, perhaps we can attribute his speedy growth to his healthy and adventurous appetite. Most children are squeamish when it comes to foods with an unusual look or texture, but not Harrison. He will eat anything that lives in water, including raw oysters on the half shell, whole fish, frogs' legs, lobster, eel, calamari tentacles and octopus.

In part because of their mutual fascination with food, Harrison and Thien have formed a very special bond. Whenever Harrison comes to Fork, he hunts Thien down to discuss his meal in depth. Harrison enjoys Fork so much that he even chose it as the destination for a class trip!

Smelts are small fish, 5 to 8 inches in length, that swim up freshwater streams to spawn in the spring. They are often eaten by salmon and sea trout. Smelts can live a long time outside water, so they can be transported a distance and still maintain their freshness.

Naturally, this trip would include a lunch for all of his classmates that he and Thien would plan together. However, when they started discussing the menu, Thien discovered that Harrison strongly believed that his eight-year-old classmates should have whole fish for lunch! As we didn't think all of the children would appreciate being served a large, whole fish, we suggested tiny, crispy smelts—one of Harrison's favorite dishes—followed by turkey sandwiches with pasta salad and brownies. Harrison was pleased, but his ideal menu would have included pan-seared frogs' legs and crispy whole striped bass.

crispy smelts with serrano-ginger pesto

Serves 4 as an appetizer

SERRANO-GINGER PESTO

4 Serrano peppers, stemmed and coarsely chopped

6 scallions, cut into 1-inch pieces

1 cup fresh cilantro leaves

2 cloves garlic, peeled

1-inch ginger root, peeled and sliced

¼ cup hazelnuts, toasted

¼ cup parmesan, grated

salt and freshly ground black pepper

2 T lime juice

⅔ cup extra-virgin olive oil

Place all ingredients from peppers to lime juice into food processor and pulse mixture until coarsely chopped. With processor running, add olive oil in a slow stream, mixing until pesto becomes a thick paste.

CRISPY SMELTS

2 cups tempura flour

1 egg

1½ cups ice-cold water

2 cups all-purpose flour

2 cups panko (Japanese bread crumbs)

1 pound (about 20) smelts, thawed if frozen, cleaned, scaled and deheaded

2 cups vegetable oil for frying

Heat oil to 365°F (check with a deep-fry thermometer) in a deep pot. In a bowl, mix tempura flour, egg and cold water. Batter should be as thin as a crêpe batter rather than thick like pancake batter. Take two separate bowls. In one, place plain flour. In the other, mix panko with 3 tablespoons plain flour. When you are nearly ready to serve and oil is hot, dredge dry smelts in flour. Next, dip into tempura batter, then panko mixture. Place smelts into oil, taking care to avoid splattering. Fry until smelts are golden brown and floating. Place fried smelts on a paper towel to drain. Serve immediately with pesto on the side.

Some adults don't want to eat frogs' legs. But some children, Harrison among them, are very open to new tastes. Perhaps the fact that frogs' legs taste like chicken will help the adults at your table become just as open to this dish, which has a Brazilian flair.

pan-seared frogs' legs with moceca sauce

Serves 4 as an appetizer

MOCECA SAUCE

1 small Spanish onion, chopped fine

3 cloves garlic, minced

3 T olive oil

1 red bell pepper cut into ½-inch cubes

¼ cup hearts of palm, cut into ½-inch cubes

1 mango, cut into ½-inch cubes

1 tomato, seeded and cut into ½-inch cubes

½ cup coconut milk

1 tsp turmeric

3 T fresh, flat-leaf parsley

salt and freshly ground black pepper

Heat oil in a medium saucepan over medium-high heat. Add garlic and onions and sauté until they are translucent. Add pepper and hearts of palm and cook an additional two minutes. Mix in mango, tomato, coconut milk, turmeric and parsley and stir to warm through. Season with salt and pepper to taste.

PAN-SEARED FROGS' LEGS

8 frogs' legs

2 cups milk

1 cup all-purpose flour

2 ounces clarified butter (see recipe in Fork Foundations)

Kosher salt and freshly ground black pepper

Marinate frogs' legs in milk for 45 minutes. Remove from milk, dredge in flour and season with salt and pepper. Heat clarified butter in a large skillet over medium-high heat. Add frogs' legs and sear for 4 to 5 minutes per side. Season to taste and serve with sauce.

Tempura flour is used to make a Japanese specialty called tempura, for which seafood or vegetables are fried in a light, golden, crispy batter. Although it might seem simple, good tempura is not easy to make. You could make your own flour but it is easier to use tempura flour. To keep the batter from becoming too glutinous and growing heavy and soggy, make it with cold or ice water.

Moceca is a Brazilian-African dish of seafood stewed with mango and coconut. Although the dish was first created by Brazilians, the Africans who arrived in Bahia, Brazil, gave it a twist by adding palm oil and coconut.

When we serve the following dish, the fish still has its head and tail but the bones are removed. At home, you can avoid bones in one of two ways: by skimming the top layer of flesh off the fish with a spoon and serving it this way, or by having a fishmonger remove only the center bone, leaving the head and tail intact.

crispy whole striped bass with sweet-and-sour sauce

Servings depend on size of fish (about 20 ounces per person)

SWEET-AND-SOUR SAUCE

1 can tomato purée

¼ cup sherry

¼ cup rice-wine vinegar

1 Spanish onion, chopped fine

2 cloves garlic, peeled, minced

¼ cup soy sauce

1 T sugar

1 T olive oil

Heat olive oil in saucepan. When pan is hot, add onions and garlic and stir until they are translucent. Add tomatoes, sherry, vinegar, soy sauce and sugar. Reduce. Keep warm and set aside.

CRISPY WHOLE STRIPED BASS

bass, scaled and cleaned

½ cup flour

1 tsp paprika

salt and freshly ground black pepper

2 cups vegetable oil for frying

On a plate, mix flour and paprika. Dredge fish with flour mixture. Season with salt and pepper. Fill a frying pan with 2 inches of oil. Heat oil until hot. Add bass, being careful about splattering. When fish floats to top, remove it and place it on paper towels to drain oil. Place fish on clean plate. Spoon sauce on top. Garnish with scallions. Serve with rice.

Kids Can Cook, Too

At age eight, Harrison was old enough to attend the joint holiday party held by his parents' companies. James' firm, Kieran Timberlake, and Meg's firm, Marguerite Rodgers, Ltd., had about 120 staff members altogether. The event took place at Fork. When Harrison arrived, he followed his normal routine: running through the restaurant to find Thien. This time, he was wearing something very special: a skullcap. A few weeks before the party, Thien had given Harrison one of his black skullcaps. But Thien was very busy preparing the hors d'oeuvres. Harrison wanted to help and would not take "No" for an answer. So we put the smallest chef's jacket we could find on Harrison and dressed him up as a line cook. Harrison helped to make mini burgers with blue cheese and caramelized onions!

3

FOURCHETTE: A BISTRO AT HEART

As I've said all along, our goal from the start was to become
a neighborhood bistro. Though by now our customers come from
well beyond the neighborhood, Fork still has a great bistro feel.
The traditional French bistro—an informal, simple restaurant that
serves wine—often features straightforward, hearty dishes such as steak
frites, roasted chicken, beef Bourguignon or French onion soup. While
our culinary interpretation of the term is a little more broad—our menu
draws upon many cuisines—we have always been a restaurant where
the food is fresh and simple, tasty and cooked to order. To me, these
qualities are fundamental to a true bistro.

When Anne-Marie was our head chef, Fork's menu was Californian in
style; under Dave, it was definitely French. While Thien's cooking has
a strong French influence as well, he is the real deal. He was trained
in France, lived in France and speaks French fluently. Of course we're
in Philadelphia, not in France, but when he took over our kitchen he
was adamant in his insistence that the kitchen be run according to the
French culinary system, which is called the brigade system. This system
dictates that the kitchen be organized into a strict hierarchy

Talented staff can work their way from prep to first line cook

of authority, responsibility and function. Since our kitchen is small, what that translated into was Thien's way or the highway. This style was hard for me to accept, since I had been schooled in management theory at Wharton and had learned all about the importance of motivating employees to perform well and feel ownership toward their jobs through participatory management. But I went with Thien's preference because I know that managing a bunch of M.B.A.s requires a different philosophy than managing restaurant employees.

A COOK IS BORN

One of the first things Thien did when he took over the kitchen was train an African prep cook named Tony Cesaire to be the night porter. When Tony arrived at Fork in 1998, he didn't speak a word of English. But one of our staff had worked with Tony's brother at another restaurant and assured us that if Tony had half the work ethic of his brother, he'd be a tremendous asset. We were short-handed in the kitchen, so Anne-Marie hired him reluctantly. I assured her that we could figure out how to work with Tony, since we had both studied French in the past (though this was not as easy as I had thought). Tony lived up to his brother's reputation until one day he disappeared without warning—behavior that is not uncommon among restaurant employees. Then, about a year later, he called me from New York to let me know that he had had difficulties with his immigration status but was returning to Philadelphia and wanted to work. Oh, and by the way, he'd left out one minor detail. His real name was Daouda Tounkara, not Tony Cesaire. We hired him back, though we still called him Tony because we were so accustomed to that name.

Eventually Tony was promoted from dishwasher to prep cook. But then he hit a plateau in his training due to our difficulty in communicating. Thus Thien's arrival was a great opportunity for Tony, as there was no longer a language barrier. As night porter, Tony came in at 11 P.M. and prepared stocks, soups and cookies and did more challenging prep jobs. Thien would meet him early in the morning to review his progress. Many staff felt that having Tony work these hours was abusive; why would anyone want to work the graveyard shift? I tried to explain that plenty of careers required unusual hours and that this opportunity was helping Tony gain Thien's trust. The strategy worked. Eventually, Tony was promoted from a seven-dollar-per-hour prep cook all the way to a salaried first line cook at thirty-thousand dollars a year. He learned how to play just about every role in Thien's kitchen, from *garde manger* to grill cook to bread maker. If that's the French system, it's not so bad.

Confit When we train our staff, we explain that confit is short for confiture, which is a preserve. Fruit confits are typically cooked and preserved in sugar. Meat confits are generally cooked and immersed in fat to preserve their shelf life. Prior to refrigeration, making confit was a way of extending the meat's freshness. Sealed and stored in a cool place, confit can last for several months. The fat on meat confit is removed prior to consumption.

Often over the course of the past several years, Thien has described his life in Paris and how much better the quality of life was there. Sometimes it has seemed as though every other sentence out of his mouth begins, "In France . . ." (pronounced *fraans*). According to him, there is no overtime in French kitchens, cooks work only thirty-nine hours a week and all cooks are members of the cooks' union. He lived in a building with a courtyard, where he and his neighbors would often have dinner parties and drink wine, regardless of whether there was an occasion to celebrate.

Finally, after listening to Thien go on about his great life in Paris, I arranged to vacation there. Although I had visited Paris before and loved it, this trip was the first one I had made since becoming a restaurateur. Of course much of our trip revolved around food. We visited open-air food markets, cafes and bistros, and naturally my friend and I had to have lunch at the brasserie where Thien had worked. For me, the highlight of the trip was our dinner at the trendy Z Kitchen Galerie, where I met Chef William LaDeuil, who had earned his reputation as chef at Guy Savoy's well-known restaurant Les Bookinistes on the Left Bank. Z Kitchen Galerie reminded me a little bit of Fork. Not that Fork can be compared to such an esteemed establishment, but the Southeastern Asian and international influences on the menu were ones I had not seen before in Paris bistros, and they appear frequently on our menu. I returned invigorated by the thought that Fork could be defined as a bistro even by French standards. Then I registered for classes at the Alliance Française to improve my French so I could eventually live in Paris. Although I've forgotten most of what I learned by now, my lessons came in handy when working with Tony and other African staff from the Côte d'Ivoire.

One of my favorite classic French bistro recipes that Thien makes is his duck confit. Usually we use duck legs. During the holidays, however, Thien will confit an entire duck for special dinners. Even though modern refrigeration makes the use of this preserving method all but obsolete, cooking duck this way still helps it keep longer, and of course the result

Paul Rodriguez, former wine manager and artist (see pages 58 and 59)

is delicious. So you can make a batch and enjoy it over the course of
a week or two. You are unlikely to get tired of it, because the number
of different ways to use duck confit is virtually endless. Besides pan
searing it and serving it with your favorite salad or sides, you can pull
it off the bone, chop it coarsely and mix it with goat cheese and parsley
to make a spread for bruschetta or flatbread (see recipe on page 97).
You can also serve it in an omelet or use the meat to make pâté. In this
recipe, the duck confit is the star of the quintessential French bistro
salad—frisée tossed with crispy bacon and a poached egg. This salad
forms a decadent finish to a tasty meal.

crispy duck confit with honey-onion marmalade and salad of frisée, bacon and poached egg

Serves 4 as a dinner first course or lunch entrée

HONEY-ONION MARMALADE

2 Spanish onions, peeled and sliced into half-moons

¼ cup extra-virgin olive oil

salt and freshly ground black pepper to taste

¼ cup honey

½ cup lemon juice

Preheat oven to 300°F. Toss onions in oil and season with salt and pepper. Spread onions on a baking sheet that has been covered with foil. Roast in oven to soften but not caramelize the onions, approximately 10 minutes. Transfer onions and their juices to a saucepan over a low flame. Stir in honey and lemon juice with a wooden spoon. Cook slowly until onions are transparent but not mushy. Let cool. (Can be made in advance and stored for up to 2 weeks in refrigerator.)

CRISPY DUCK CONFIT

4 duck legs

1 sprig fresh thyme

1 sprig fresh rosemary

1 sprig fresh tarragon

1 T Kosher or sea salt

1 star anise

⅛ tsp whole cloves

⅛ tsp black peppercorns

1 cup duck fat

½ cup butter

½ cup olive oil

½ to 1 tsp olive oil for searing

salt and freshly ground black pepper

Preheat oven to 250°F. Place duck legs in an 8-inch square baking dish. Add herbs, spices and salt. Melt duck fat, butter and olive oil together in a saucepan. Pour mixture over duck. Transfer pan with duck to oven and roast 2 to 2½ hours or until meat pulls away from femur. Remove pan from oven and let fat cool. Remove duck from oil using clean tongs. (The duck can be made in advance and stored in the refrigerator for up to 2 weeks. The oil can be strained through a fine-mesh strainer or a chinois and saved for future use.)

When you are ready to enjoy this salad, heat a sauté pan over high heat. Add olive oil to coat pan. Season duck with salt and pepper. Place duck skin-side down on hot pan. Some of the fat will help sear duck. Reduce heat to medium. When outside is crispy, turn leg and sear other side. Remove from heat and keep warm.

SALAD

3 cups frisée

12 ounces vinaigrette of your choice

1 T cooked bacon or prosciutto bits

4 eggs

2 T white vinegar

Toss frisée with dressing. Divide among 4 plates and sprinkle each salad with bacon bits. Fill medium pot with water and stir in white vinegar. Bring to a simmer over medium-high heat. Reduce heat to medium-low, crack eggs one at a time and drop immediately into water. Let eggs simmer about 2 minutes, until whites are cooked but yolks are still runny. Gently lift eggs out one at a time with a slotted spoon. After lifting out each egg, set spoon on a towel or paper towel for a moment to soak up extra water. Then place egg on top of a plate of salad. Continue until done. Prop a duck leg against each salad. Put a tablespoon of marmalade on each plate. Serve immediately.

Mark Fisher and Thien at a "soignée affair" celebrating the birthdays of our dear friends Otto Tidwell (not shown) and D

soignée

Soignée is the French term Thien uses whenever I tell him there are members of the press, dignitaries, celebrities or regular customers in the house. It's an adjective that means "fancy" as well as a form of a verb that means "to care for." As a server, if you hear him using the word, you expect that Thien will make the food for that table and/or create a special *amuse bouche* (a bite-sized amusement for the mouth) for the occasion.

Thien doesn't call his amusements by that name, though; he prefers the term *amuse gueule*. Amuse bouche is the term used most in upscale, refined restaurants. Though similar in concept, an amuse gueule is literally a bite-sized morsel meant for the mouth of an animal rather than that of a person! The French use this term in a playful way; it refers to a tidbit that has no boundaries with regard to the menu. At Fork, it affords our chef the freedom to express his creativity with whatever ingredients we have in house.

Thien's Grilled Shrimp with Poblano-Cucumber Relish on Tostada is an example of the many amuses gueules he has created over the years. The Poblano-Cucumber Relish might be used on a single oyster or placed alongside a single escargot stuffed into a shell with crabmeat, ginger and butter. Regardless of whether the amuse he creates is French, Asian or Latino in origin, it is Thien's way of expressing hospitality.

A tostada is a crispy, flat tortilla that is either toasted or deep fried. Used widely in Mexican cuisine, tostadas are often served with chopped lettuce, sour cream and salsa.

grilled shrimp with poblano-cucumber relish on tostada

Makes 16 to 20 as an amuse gueule or 4 as an appetizer

POBLANO-CUCUMBER RELISH

1 poblano pepper, seeded and diced small

1 cucumber, seeded and diced small

½ cup red onion, minced

¼ cup lime juice

1 tsp cumin

1 cup fresh cilantro, chopped

¼ cup olive oil

¼ cup lime juice

½ tsp sugar

1 tsp salt

freshly ground black pepper

Combine all ingredients in a large bowl.

GRILLED SHRIMP

16 to 20 large shrimp, peeled and deveined

¼ cup olive oil

salt and black pepper

Preheat grill. Toss shrimp and olive oil together and season with salt and pepper. Place shrimp on hot grill grates and grill about 1 minute per side, just until pink.

TOSTADA

ten 10-inch corn tortillas

2 cups corn oil

Heat oil to about 365°F in a deep saucepan or Dutch oven over medium-high heat. Using a 2-inch round cookie cutter, cut 2 circles out of each tortilla. (If you are using the recipe to make an appetizer, you can cut 4-inch circles instead.) Drop tortilla rounds in batches into hot oil and fry just until golden. Remove from oil and transfer to a cooling rack lined with paper towels. Sprinkle with salt and pepper.

Spoon 2 teaspoons of cucumber-poblano relish on each round. Top with grilled shrimp and garnish with baby greens. Serve with sour cream or guacamole (see recipe on page 228).

Since we almost always have duck confit in the house, it is a logical ingredient for us to use for an amuse gueule, especially since it is so popular and is not easily replicated at home. The duck legs can be shredded to make duck rillettes, which combine well with many ingredients to create a delicious start to a meal.

duck rillettes with goat cheese on flatbread

Serves 4 to 6 as an appetizer or a light lunch

2 duck confit legs (recipe on page 97)

4 ounces Montrachet-style
  goat cheese

fresh parsley

salt and freshly ground black pepper
  to taste

Shred duck off bone into bowl. Add goat cheese, parsley, salt and pepper. Gently mix. Spread onto toast points, crackers, grilled bread or crudités. Garnish with baby greens, parsley or chervil.

One of the biggest compliments someone can pay to a restaurant is to hold their wedding reception there. It is a tremendous honor to be included in plans that are so important in the lives of people you know; it's the ultimate in soignée. John Ellis and Audrey Wilson have had a standing reservation at Fork every Friday night at 7 P.M. for the past ten years. When they booked their wedding reception with us, we wondered what we could possibly do to make their reception extra special, especially since I knew the ceremony would be over the top.

The ceremony was held at Christ Church, one of the country's oldest churches. John is a jazz musician and Audrey loves opera and art, so their wedding ceremony included a concert performed by some of the most talented classical musicians in the area, including performers from the Philadelphia Orchestra. Barbara Dever, an internationally renowned opera diva, sang Ave Maria. Audrey was stunning in her red satin Italian gown, and her gorgeous nieces, the bridesmaids, were all dressed in white.

Audrey designed the menu for the reception and included some of her favorites, but Thien added special touches to make it an exceptional dinner. One of the things Audrey insisted upon was a salad with Thien's gribiche dressing, a classic French sauce that consists of an herb vinaigrette with chopped egg. (If you don't eat eggs, they can be deleted easily.) We couldn't give Audrey the everyday salad from our menu, so Thien used gribiche in this appetizer to accompany the most succulent sea scallops he could find, as well as shaved black truffles, which she also loves.

Diver sea scallops are sea scallops that are hand picked by divers. Compared to scallops harvested by boats, diver scallops tend to be larger and less gritty.

Gribiche, or sauce gribiche, is a classic French sauce used as a condiment or a dressing for salads, cooked vegetables (asparagus or leeks), fish, poultry or eggs. It was named after a famous French general and was especially popular served with a calf's head. Gribiche is made with shallots, fresh parsley, cornichons, capers, hard-boiled eggs, oil, vinegar and seasonings. However, other ingredients are often added, such as chives, more herbs and prepared mustard. Although the ingredients for gribiche are similar to those in tartar sauce, the oil and vinegar are not emulsified for gribiche. In the summertime, I love gribiche dressing with poached or smoked salmon. It can be a great accompaniment to tuna, chicken or any salad as well.

pan-seared diver sea scallops with beets, black truffles and gribiche

Serves 4 as a dinner appetizer

GRIBICHE DRESSING

½ cup shallot, chopped fine

¼ cup capers

¼ cup cornichons, chopped fine

½ cup fresh parsley, chopped fine

½ cup fresh chives, chopped fine

¼ cup fresh tarragon, chopped fine

¼ cup fresh chervil, chopped fine

1 T fresh thyme, chopped fine

zest of 1 lemon

¾ cup freshly squeezed lemon juice

1-1/2 cups extra-virgin olive oil

1 tsp Kosher salt

¼ tsp freshly ground black pepper

4 hard-boiled eggs, peeled and coarsely chopped (optional)

Whisk all ingredients together and adjust seasoning if necessary. Store in refrigerator until ready to use (can be refrigerated for several weeks). Remove dressing from refrigerator 20 minutes before using to allow oil to come to room temperature. Whisk again to emulsify oil and lemon juice. Add egg if desired. However, if you wish to store any remaining dressing, do not add egg to entire batch. Remainder can then be stored in an airtight container and refrigerated for up to 2 weeks.

PAN-SEARED DIVER SEA SCALLOPS

1 T olive oil

8 diver sea scallops (approximately ¾ to 1 pound)

Kosher salt

freshly ground black pepper

1 to 2 beets, roasted and quartered (see page 72 for instructions on roasting beets)

2 tsp black truffle peelings or fresh truffle shavings

Pat scallops dry and season with salt and pepper. Heat olive oil in a large sauté pan over medium-high heat until oil is hot but not smoking. Sear scallops in pan, about 2 minutes on each side. Arrange scallops and beets on a plate. Drizzle with Gribiche Dressing and sprinkle with black truffle peelings.

the cook and the gardener

Beyond such special occasions, the day-to-day bistro menu reflects the cooking techniques and ingredients Thien learned to use in France. Most dishes are extremely simple and seasonal. Like French country cooking, Fork's menu is often inspired by local produce, and Fork works closely with local farmers. Thien has a particular kinship with the owners of Branch Creek Farm, with whom he has become great friends, and our menu is often shaped by what the Dornstreichs are growing. Judy calls on Mondays and Thursdays to give Thien the rundown on what is good, available and plentiful.

Since Mark and Judy have been such great friends and influencers of Fork since the beginning, I decided to have a harvest dinner centered around Branch Creek's produce. Mark suggested contacting Amanda Hesser, the *New York Times* columnist who authored the award-winning book *The Cook and the Gardener*. The book describes both her experiences with food and her relationships with other people— in particular with a tough French gardener who took care of the vegetables and herbs at Château Fey in Burgundy, where she stayed for a year. We built an evening around her book and featured Mark and Judy as the farmers whose growing season and crop choices have often influenced our menu. Amanda joined us for a special book dinner in September 2003 after the release of her second book, *Cooking for Mr. Latté*.

Judy and Mark Dornstreich, Branch Creek Farm

This recipe reminds me of Amanda because it uses celery root and fennel, which were readily available in her château garden in the fall. Jerusalem artichokes weren't in her garden, but they taste fresh and summery. Also called sunchokes, Jerusalem artichokes come from sunflower roots and are nothing like their Mediterranean namesake. They can be served raw or cooked. When raw, they are like a cross between jicama and a potato. They give a nice crunch to this dish.

prosciutto-wrapped rainbow trout stuffed with jerusalem artichokes with lemon oil and celery-root fennel slaw

Serves 4 as a dinner main course

LEMON OIL

peel of 3 lemons

juice of 1 lemon

½ cup extra-virgin olive oil

Blend in food processor to emulsify. Set aside.

JERUSALEM ARTICHOKES

½ cup Jerusalem artichokes, peeled and julienned

1 sprig of fresh thyme

1 T olive oil

salt and freshly ground black pepper

Heat a sauté pan over high heat. Add olive oil. When pan is hot, add artichokes and thyme. Sauté approximately 5 minutes, stirring frequently. Season with salt and pepper.

CELERY-ROOT FENNEL SLAW

½ celery root, peeled and julienned

½ fennel bulb, shaved using a mandoline

1 T fresh flat-leaf parsley, chopped

½ red onion, sliced into half moons

1 T extra-virgin olive oil

1 tsp lemon juice

salt and freshly ground black pepper to taste

Toss all ingredients together when ready to serve.

PROSCIUTTO-WRAPPED RAINBOW TROUT

4 whole rainbow trout, deboned and deheaded

8 pieces of prosciutto di Parma, sliced thin

1 lime, sliced into rounds

4 sprigs fresh thyme

baby greens

salt and freshly ground black pepper to taste

Place stuffing, 3 lime slices and a sprig of thyme inside trout. Wrap each trout with 2 slices of prosciutto. Lightly season trout with salt and pepper. In a hot pan with a ½ tsp of oil, sear trout, 4 to 6 minutes on each side.

To assemble, divide Celery-Root Fennel Slaw among 4 plates. Place trout alongside slaw. Drizzle lemon oil around plate. Garnish with baby greens and serve immediately.

Since its beginning, Fork has supported local farming and artisanal food
production. So naturally we joined Slow Food soon after we opened.
Slow Food is an international organization that promotes sustainable
agriculture and ecologically sound and traditional food production
and that honors food as a builder and sustainer of community. When
we were approached by the local chapter to host an event, we jumped
at the opportunity, especially since the dinner would raise funds to
sponsor Mark and Judy's trip to Terra Madre. Terra Madre is an event
in Piedmont, Italy, that brings together thousands of small-scale food
producers from all over the world to share ideas and discuss solutions
to the challenges of their work.

Yet the dinner was scheduled for late September. The difficulty with
making a harvest dinner at this time in the northeastern United States is
that you risk the possibility of frost damaging the crops you intend
to serve. And Branch Creek Farm is one hour north of Philadelphia,
which makes it about ten degrees cooler. Up there, late-summer
vegetables such as tomatoes, eggplant and zucchini are on their last legs
by late September. So we based our dinner around fall produce, including
squash, pears and apples. This recipe takes advantage of a variety of
heirloom pear called Vermont Beauty, which is yellowish-caramel in color.
But you can substitute another variety of pear, such as Bartlett.

pan-seared duck breast with port-poached vermont beauty pears, butternut-squash mash and sautéed beet greens

Serves 4 as a dinner main course

PORT-POACHED VERMONT BEAUTY PEARS

2 sprigs fresh thyme

2 sprigs fresh rosemary

3 cups port

4 Vermont Beauty or Bartlett pears

¼ cup lemon juice

¼ cup honey

salt and freshly ground black pepper

Combine port and honey in a medium pot over high heat. Add pears and herbs and bring liquid to a boil over high heat. Reduce heat to medium-low and simmer 30 to 40 minutes, until pears are tender. Remove pot from heat and allow pears and poaching liquid to cool before refrigerating. Leave pears in poaching liquid until you are ready to serve them.

BUTTERNUT-SQUASH MASH

2 pounds butternut squash, peeled, seeded and cut into 1-inch cubes

2 T olive oil

2 pounds Idaho potatoes

½ cup heavy cream

½ stick (2 ounces) butter

1 T Kosher salt

freshly ground black pepper

Preheat oven to 375°F. Toss squash with olive oil and sprinkle with salt and pepper. Spread out on a baking sheet lined with aluminum foil. Transfer to oven along with whole potatoes and roast until tender—30 to 40 minutes for squash, 45 minutes to 1 hour for potatoes. Stir squash cubes occasionally to avoid browning on sides. When fork tender, split potatoes down middle and scoop out inside from skins. Combine potato with squash in a bowl.

Meanwhile, melt butter with cream in a small saucepan. Pour mixture over vegetables. Add salt and pepper and mash with a hand masher or whip with a mixer on medium speed until mixture is almost smooth. Adjust seasoning to taste.

PORT SAUCE

2 cups port

2 cups meat stock (see recipe in Fork Foundations or use store-bought)

Reduce to 1 cup of liquid over high heat.

PAN-SEARED DUCK BREAST

4 duck breasts

1 T olive oil

Preheat oven to 450°F. Score skin side of duck breasts, taking care not to cut through the meat. Season each breast with salt and pepper. Heat olive oil in a large pan over high heat. Place duck skin-side down and sear until skin is crisp, about 5 minutes. Turn breasts over and transfer to oven. Roast about 5 minutes for medium rare. Remove duck from pan and tent with foil until ready to serve.

BEET GREENS

2 cups beet greens (from Lutz green-leaf beets, if possible), cleaned

1 clove garlic, minced

1 T olive oil

salt and freshly ground black pepper to taste

Heat oil in pan. When pan is hot, add garlic. Reduce heat if necessary so as not to burn garlic. Add beet greens and cook until they are wilted.

To serve, slice the duck breasts in thin strips. Place 1 large spoonful of mashed potatoes in individual pasta bowls. Place duck on one side and a poached pear and greens on the other. Drizzle sauce over duck, pears and potatoes.

mixed farm lettuce, lutz green-leaf beets, gorgonzola and candied pecans with green-peppercorn vinaigrette

Serves 4 as a dinner appetizer or lunch entrée

CANDIED PECANS

1 pound pecan or walnut halves

2 quarts water

2½ cups sugar

1 cup water

4 cups vegetable or canola oil

Bring 2 quarts of water to a boil in a medium saucepot. Blanch pecans for 2 minutes. Drain in colander. Rinse with cold water and drain thoroughly. Combine sugar with 1 cup cold water in a small, heavy saucepot. Bring to boil, reduce heat and simmer 2 to 3 minutes or until sugar is completely dissolved. Add pecans, stir and cook 5 minutes in syrup. While pecans are cooking, heat oil in saucepot over medium heat until hot, approximately 3 minutes.

Using a slotted spoon, take pecans out of syrup, drain excess syrup and put into hot oil. Keep stirring pecans, watching to make sure nuts don't burn and turning heat down if necessary. Cook until medium dark brown (7 to 8 minutes). Remove with a slotted spoon and cool on cookie tray. When nuts are cool, remove excess oil using paper towels. Store in airtight container.

SALAD

2 large heads soft farm lettuce, washed and dried

4 medium Lutz green-leaf beets, roasted and peeled (see roasting instructions on page 72) and quartered

¼ cup Italian Gorgonzola dolce or Gorgonzola cremificato

¼ cup Green-Peppercorn Vinaigrette (recipe on page 72)

¼ cup candied pecans

Gently toss lettuce with vinaigrette in a bowl. Place greens on plates. Divide beets up between plates equally. Sprinkle with cheese and candied pecans.

Green peppercorns are under-ripe peppercorn berries. To preserve their green color, these peppercorns are usually kept in brine, which deactivates the enzyme that turns them black. They can be freeze dried to the same effect.

After offering beets consistently on the menu for the past ten years, I have come to the conclusion that people either love beets or hate them. Beets have an earthy flavor with a hint of sweetness when at their peak, which is generally between June and October, but they are plentiful year round. Lutz green-leaf beets are an heirloom variety of red beet. But as their name indicates, they have green leaves, which can be used as a substitute for sautéed spinach or Swiss chard.

Fresh, local salad ingredients are crucial to the taste of this salad, but the real secret to its taste is the candied pecans, which are made according to my mother's recipe. Although the concept of caramelized pecans is simple, it is very difficult to replicate how nicely browned and crispy she makes them. This recipe has been perfected over twenty years, and she always makes a batch for holiday gifts in our family. The nuts are for sale in Fork:etc, hand cooked by my mom!

Anise hyssop is a perennial herb that Judy loves to grow. Often we use the edible violet flowers for colorful garnishes on dessert. The herb is in the mint family but exudes an anise-like aroma. Here we use it in a homemade sorbet. Making sorbet is easy, and you can make it in small batches with just about any fresh herb, such as mint or basil.

anise-hyssop sorbet with lemon-thyme cookies

Makes approximately 6 to 8 servings

ANISE-HYSSOP SORBET

2 cups water

1 cup sugar

1 cup fresh anise hyssop leaves

2 T lemon juice

In a medium saucepan, bring water and sugar to a boil. Simmer until sugar is dissolved. Add anise hyssop, turn off heat, cover and let it infuse into the mixture for 20 minutes. Strain flavored syrup and cool in refrigerator until it is completely chilled. Stir in lemon juice, pour syrup into ice-cream maker and follow manufacturer's instructions to finish.

LEMON-THYME COOKIES

1 stick butter, room temperature

½ cup plus 2 T sugar

1 tsp vanilla extract

¼ tsp lemon extract

⅓ cup fresh lemon thyme, chopped fine

¼ tsp salt

1 large egg

1¼ cup all-purpose flour

Beat butter and sugar with an electric mixer until light and fluffy. Add vanilla, lemon extract, lemon thyme and salt, mixing until combined. Beat in egg. Add flour and beat until just blended. Place dough on a sheet of plastic wrap. Shape dough into an 8-inch log. Wrap with plastic wrap and chill for at least 2 hours.

Preheat oven to 350°F. Line a baking sheet with parchment paper or a Silpat. Cut log crosswise into ¼-inch thick slices. Transfer cookies to prepared baking sheets and bake until cookies are golden around the edges, about 10 to 13 minutes. (Recipe makes about 2 dozen cookies.) Allow cookies to cool slightly, then remove from baking sheet and cool further on a rack.

To serve, place a scoop or two of sorbet in a bowl and place one or two cookies on the side. Garnish with a sprig of anise hyssop, if desired.

bistro cooking

French bistro cuisine is known for its heartiness and richness, and many dishes include butter and cream. The thing I love most about Thien's French cooking is that he rarely uses butter or cream. Perhaps it is his Vietnamese background that makes him avoid these key ingredients. To me, the omission makes his bistro food taste more true to form; the essence of a bistro is its informality, which should make it a place for everyday dining. As a person who dines out seven days a week, I can only take so many heavy dishes. Of course cream and butter do make food taste rich and decadent, but from a health perspective I can easily do without them.

Rarely does Thien thicken a soup with cream. As a result, when he makes soups, we often have to explain to guests that the soup contains no dairy. Usually he uses potato, barley, rice, sweet potato or some other starch to create a smooth, creamy texture. But more often than not, customers are excited to try his renditions of classically dairy-rich soups. This Wild-Mushroom Bisque has always been one of the most popular.

wild mushroom bisque

Serves 4 to 6

1 pound wild mushrooms (oyster, crimini, shiitake, portobella and so on)

¼ cup olive oil

2 T butter or olive oil

1 small onion, diced small

3 cloves garlic, minced

½ cup chopped carrot

1 celery stalk, diced small

½ fennel bulb, diced small

6 cups (48 ounces) vegetable stock or water

½ cup barley

1 T Kosher salt

½ tsp freshly ground black pepper

1 T rice-wine or white-wine vinegar.

Preheat oven to 375°F. Rinse mushrooms under cool, running water and pat dry. Trim any tough, woody stems. Toss mushrooms with olive oil, salt and pepper. Spread them out on a rimmed baking sheet lined with foil or sprayed with cooking oil. Roast in oven for 15 minutes.

Melt butter or heat olive oil in a Dutch oven or large pot over medium heat. Add onion, garlic, carrot, celery and fennel and sauté until slightly caramelized, about 10 minutes. Deglaze pan with ½ cup vegetable stock and then add remaining cups of stock. Stir in roasted mushrooms and barley and cook until barley is tender, about 30 minutes.

Transfer mixture in batches to food processor or blender and purée soup (you can use an immersion blender instead, if you prefer). Return to pot, add salt and pepper to taste and reheat to serve. Add water, if necessary, to create desired consistency.

How to Pan Sear Fish

When you are pan searing fish, pay attention to the temperature of the pan and the fat so that a good crust will form. If the pan is too hot, the outside of the fish will burn and the inside will be undercooked. If there is not enough heat, the fish will absorb the cooking fat, resulting in a greasy flavor. Here is a good method to use: Heat olive oil or butter over moderate heat. Just as oil begins to smoke or butter to foam, place fish filets into pan, skin-side up. Cook over medium heat to create a seared crust, which will make it easy to flip fish over. Carefully flip, reduce heat and continue cooking over low heat. As a guideline, allow 10 minutes total for each inch of thickness. To test for doneness, press with your finger. Fish should be firm, not flaky.

citrus-crusted wild striped bass with roasted tomato and garlic sauce, orzo salad and sautéed snap peas

Serves 4 as a dinner main course

ROASTED TOMATO AND GARLIC SAUCE

12 plum tomatoes

2 sprigs fresh thyme

6 cloves garlic

¼ cup olive oil

salt and freshly ground black pepper

1 T lemon juice

1 tsp honey

Preheat oven to 375°F. Toss all ingredients except lemon juice in a bowl. Place on a baking sheet and roast until skins of tomatoes break, about 20 minutes. Transfer roasted ingredients to a food processor and purée with lemon juice and additional salt and pepper to taste. Set aside.

CITRUS CRUST

1 T lemon zest

1 T lime zest

1 T orange zest

¼ cup fresh parsley, chopped fine

¼ cup fresh cilantro, chopped fine

¼ cup grated Parmigiano Reggiano

salt and freshly ground black pepper to taste

Combine all ingredients and refrigerate.

ORZO SALAD

½ pound orzo pasta

3 scallions, sliced thin

1 red pepper, cored, seeded and chopped fine

1 red onion, chopped fine

¼ cup each chopped fresh mint and cilantro

2½ T lemon juice

½ cup olive oil

salt and freshly ground black pepper to taste

Cook pasta according to manufacturer's directions and cool. Prep other ingredients.

Combine all ingredients in a large mixing bowl and toss. Taste and adjust seasoning.

WILD STRIPED BASS

4 filets of wild striped bass

salt and freshly ground black pepper

olive oil

Preheat oven to 350°F. Season fish with salt and pepper. Heat an ovenproof pan over high heat. Add olive oil and sear fish with skin side up for about 3 minutes. Flip over and place fish in oven until cooked.

SAUTÉED SNAP PEAS

2 cups snap peas, cleaned

1 clove garlic, minced

1 T olive oil

salt and freshly ground black pepper
  to taste

Heat oil in pan. When pan is hot,
add garlic. Add snap peas and cook
until they are tender. Reduce heat
if necessary so as not to burn garlic.

To assemble, warm sauce if necessary.
Place sauce on plate. Scoop one large
spoonful of orzo onto each plate.
Place snap peas to the side. Set fish
skin-side up over orzo and peas
and cover with crust. Garnish with
baby greens.

Particularly when it comes to fish, I prefer a lighter style. Black bass is
one of my favorite fish, but it has just two brief seasons, in spring and
early autumn. Its skin bears a pattern that looks like houndstooth plaid,
and its taste is mild and flaky. Originally this recipe called for black bass,
but wild striped bass (also called rockfish) is more readily available to us
and offers a great alternative.

Jicama is a crisp, slightly sweet tuber grown mostly in Texas, South America and Mexico. Its starchy roots are similar in texture to the water chestnut. Jicama can be stored uncovered in a cool, dry place for up to three weeks. Once cut, it may be wrapped in plastic and stored in the refrigerator for about seven days. Keep in mind, however, that the starch begins to convert to sugar over time.

Another light fish dish that could become a daily habit for me is seared, herb-crusted tuna. It is important to go to a reputable source for the freshest, highest-quality tuna. Good ahi tuna should have a deep red color, like the color of cassis. If it's grey or too pink, it may have been frozen. You can serve this dish with just about anything. For lunch, it works well as a part of a Niçoise salad; for dinner, roasted potatoes and vegetables make ideal accompaniments. In the summertime, we serve this tuna as an entrée on top of slices of tomatoes, potatoes, beets, fennel or artichokes, drizzled with a Thai-basil vinaigrette.

seared, herb-crusted ahi tuna with jicama-scallion slaw

Serves 4 as an appetizer or 2 as a light lunch

HERB CRUST

2 T dried oregano

2 tsp dried rosemary

1 tsp ground cumin

1 tsp coriander seed

2 tsp fennel seed

1 tsp mustard seed

1 tsp sugar

1 tsp black peppercorns

1 tsp white peppercorns

1 tsp Kosher salt

Mix all ingredients together and grind in coffee grinder. Set aside.

JICAMA-SCALLION SLAW

1 large jicama, peeled and julienned

4 scallions, cut into 3-inch pieces and julienned

½ bunch fresh, flat-leaf parsley, chiffonade

½ red onion, sliced into half moons

2 T fresh lemon juice

2 T rice-wine vinegar

2 T extra-virgin olive oil

salt and pepper

Mix all ingredients together. Drain liquid when serving.

SEARED AHI TUNA

½ to ¾ pound fresh, sushi-grade ahi tuna loin

1 T extra-virgin olive oil or butter

Trim any darkened meat and skin off tuna. Cover tuna evenly with herb mixture. Blacken butter or heat oil in a nonstick pan over high heat. Sear all sides equally, approximately 30 seconds on each side, being careful not to overcook. Remove from heat. Using a sharp knife, cut into thin ¼-inch slices. Assemble tuna on plates. Serve with slaw on the side. Garnish with baby greens.

On rare occasions, a more decadent dish does appear on Fork's menu. These dishes are always extremely popular. This recipe is the perfect springtime dish, as it features morel mushrooms, which appear usually in May, and asparagus, which is also best in early spring.

Morels are highly porous mushrooms that come into season in the spring. Prized in French cuisine, they are usually dark and oval in shape.

pan-roasted halibut with beurre blanc, morels, onions and asparagus tips aside saffron basmati rice

Serves 4 as a dinner main course

BEURRE BLANC

See recipe on page 20.

SAFFRON BASMATI RICE

2 T olive oil

1 cup chopped onion

2 cloves garlic, minced

1½ cups basmati rice

3 cups water

1 tsp salt

¼ tsp saffron

Preheat oven to 300°F. Heat oil in a large, nonstick saucepan over medium-high heat. Add onion and garlic and sauté until they are soft. Stir in rice to coat it with oil. Add water, salt and saffron. Cover saucepan and transfer to oven. Bake for 25 minutes. Remove pan from oven and fluff rice with fork. Season with additional salt and black pepper to taste.

PAN-ROASTED HALIBUT

4 halibut filets, approximately 6 to 8 ounces each

2 T olive oil

salt and freshly ground black pepper

Heat pan. Add oil. When oil is hot, carefully place halibut filets into pan. When fish detaches from pan and browns, turn over. Continue searing until fish is cooked through, approximately 5 minutes.

MORELS, ONIONS AND ASPARAGUS TIPS

1 T butter

8 fresh morels

½ cup asparagus tips

1 Spanish onion, chopped

Melt butter in a sauté pan over medium-high heat. When butter sizzles, add onions and sauté until they are translucent. Add asparagus tips and morels, sautéing until tender.

Put rice on plate. Place halibut to side. Top with sautéed vegetables. Drizzle warm beurre blanc over halibut. Garnish with baby greens.

Part of European tradition is enjoying a glass of wine with dinner. Usually on Sundays we have our weekly wine tasting, and Roberto also graciously brings in a great bottle from his wine cellar. Then one day Thien added a new excitement to the evening. Knowing we would be drinking well, he said to us, "I want to cook for you on Sunday nights. You're the owners; you should be eating something special. I would love to do it." Again, soignée. Roberto, always up for a great meal, was certainly not going to say no and gladly offered to pair the meal with his personal wine! But I felt squeamish. I didn't want to eat foods that customers couldn't order off the menu. Thien said, "If they want it, they can order it, too!" Suddenly, Sundays had taken on a new twist.

At first we used these Sunday nights to develop and test new menu ideas. The first few dinners started out that way and included unusual dishes such as steamed clams and eel with tomato and watercress and roasted ring-necked dove with sauce chasseur. Often, new ideas from Sunday's experiments would go on the menu the very next day. Fork sushi, for instance, began one Sunday night and became a popular menu item. Thien makes traditional sushi rolls but incorporates twists, such as substituting crispy baked rice for sushi rice or creating a sushi roll with fresh rice noodles.

One Sunday dinner included live shrimp that were to be cooked at the table. Before dinner, Thien put them on ice to numb their reflexes. He then made a delicious herb broth with rosemary, thyme, garlic, shallots and olive oil. Large bowls of Thien's steeping broth came out, topped with olive oil to seal the broth and keep it warm. The shrimp were then bathed in the hot broth to cook them. As these newly awakened shrimp were added to the bowls, some began to regain their senses and used their survival instincts to leap out! As our meal progressed, the remaining shrimp woke from their ice-induced coma, and some went leaping in all directions. It was quite a sight, to say the least. Roberto thought that this would make an incredibly memorable experience for a colleague of his and insisted that they be served at the friend's retirement dinner, as well as at a dinner for his nephews, who ranged in age from three to twelve at the time. You can imagine their delight.

Thien rarely eats the Sunday dinner he prepares. Usually he just sits with us and drinks wine. We always beg him to eat, but he has explained that, while he loves watching us enjoy our dinner, he doesn't eat his own food in front of guests. Why? Because if we say that the food is good and he agrees, then his behavior would be too narcissistic.

fishermen

Thien has often envisioned a day when he would come over to someone's house, knock on the door holding a freshly killed rabbit by the ears, and cook it up for the family. To me, cooking anything freshly caught is so French. There are no rabbits being cooked at Fork, but on numerous occasions we have had the luxury of serving freshly caught fish that were rushed to the restaurant just hours after being caught. The simplest preparations are always best.

I have been lucky to know both Wayne Aretz, my boyfriend, and his brother Bob, who created the brand identity for Fork. They are both avid fishermen, and often they bring back their catch for us to enjoy. I still remember one of the first times we got a fresh catch at Fork. One Sunday afternoon, Bob called me unexpectedly at about 4:00, and I could hear the excitement in his voice. He was driving back from Long Beach Island and had caught two large striped bass off the Atlantic coast while surf fishing. He was calling to see if we wanted to prepare and eat them together at the restaurant.

I told Thien immediately about Bob's offer, and he became just as excited as Bob. These two fish, from Bob's description, were clearly not the one- to one-and-a-half-pounders we get at the restaurant; it sounded as though they were ten- to fifteen-pound fish. When Bob arrived, he opened his ice chest and showed me his prizes. Their skin was glistening, their eyes were glossy and their blood was red. I called my friends on the phone in a last-minute effort to assemble a dinner party of about ten people. Then Thien cleaned and prepared the fish for an incredible meal. When fish is that fresh, it only needs the simplest preparation. He filled it with lemon

Thien and the striped bass Bob caught

Bob Aretz and Thien after eating Bob's catch

slices, thyme and lemon thyme, then simply rubbed the outsides with olive oil, salt and pepper. He served them to us on a giant platter so we could appreciate the size of the fish. When cooking whole fish at home, you must use the hottest grill possible and rub the fish with oil; otherwise, the skin will stick to the grill. Here is the recipe.

grilled whole striped bass

Number of servings depends on size of fish; allow 1½ pounds per person

1 cup olive oil

1 to 2 lemons, sliced into thin rounds

1 bunch fresh thyme

1 bunch fresh lemon thyme

1 whole striped bass, cleaned and scaled

salt and freshly ground black pepper to taste

Preheat grill. Brush grill grates with oil. Rub outside of fish generously with olive oil. Rub outside of fish with thyme and lemon thyme. Place herbs and lemon in fish cavity. When grill is at its hottest, place fish on oiled grates. Let fish cook without turning, 5 minutes for each pound. Gently turn fish. Cook to desired doneness.

The only exception to Thien's rule about not eating with us on Sunday nights (see sidebar on page 116) comes when he manages to get really fresh Dungeness crabs from his neighbor. Sometimes, the first course will be a decadent bowl of *fruits de mer*—shrimp or langoustines, oysters and sometimes clams on the half shell and, when he is feeling really decadent, whole Maine lobsters. At times, the amount of seafood he serves is embarrassing! One or two staff members will parade to our table, carrying a gigantic ceramic bowl filled with crushed ice and fruits de mer.

Usually on these occasions we eat the fruits de mer with just a few squeezes of lemon, Champagne Mignonette and, on rare occasion, Wasabi Cocktail Sauce. This shrimp cocktail recipe gives the basic method for poaching any shellfish.

Wasabi is a root that is often referred to as Japanese horseradish. It is served aside sushi and recognized for its strong, mustardy flavor, which burns the nasal passages rather than the tongue. Fresh wasabi root must be grated fine. Wasabi is also available in paste or powder forms.

poached shrimp with wasabi cocktail sauce

Serves 8 to 10 as an appetizer or hors d'oeuvre

WASABI COCKTAIL SAUCE

2 T lemon juice

1½ T wasabi powder

½ cup ketchup

Stir wasabi powder into lemon juice to dissolve it. Mix in ketchup to combine all ingredients.

POACHING LIQUID

water

1 Spanish onion, halved

8 cloves of garlic

1 sprig fresh rosemary

1 sprig fresh thyme

3 fresh parsley stems

1 lemon, halved

1 tsp salt

3 T Cajun seasoning

3 T olive oil

1 cup white wine

2 pounds jumbo shrimp, peeled and deveined

Fill a large pot about two-thirds of the way with water. Add remaining ingredients and bring to a boil. Drop in shrimp and let cook for about 3 minutes, just until pink. Drain shrimp, run under cold water and arrange on platter filled with crushed ice. Place a dish of Wasabi Cocktail Sauce in the center of the platter and serve.

Oysters are generally labeled by the location where they were farmed. There are five basic varieties—the Belon type, which are sweet and briny; the Olympia type, which are farmed primarily on the Puget Sound in Washington; the Japanese variety, such as Kumamotos, which are creamy and buttery; the Portuguese variety and the Blue Point variety, which are native to America. Typically at Fork we carry Long Island Blue Points, West Coast Emerald Cove or Gigamoto oysters.

My last trip to Paris just happened to coincide with the season for Brittany Belon oysters. Brittany Belon oysters are considered by many to be the perfect type for eating on the half shell. Apparently they were so plentiful in the early twentieth century that oysters were considered a poor man's food! If I can't get away to Paris, my favorite place to enjoy oysters is at the bar with a big bistro plateau at Balthazar in New York City. Here is a recipe—along with some guidance on buying and opening oysters—so you can enjoy wonderful oysters at home.

How to Buy Oysters

Raw oysters, or any shellfish for that matter, should always be purchased from a reputable fishmonger or seafood store. A strong, fishy odor in the store is not a good sign. Check the shipper's tag that shows that the oysters were properly harvested and that the harvester, processor or shipper is certified by the government. Finally, examine the oysters before buying them; live oysters will have closed or slightly open shells.

oysters on the half shell
with champagne mignonette

CHAMPAGNE MIGNONETTE

1 cup Champagne
   or white-wine vinegar

2 T olive oil

2 T lemon juice

¼ tsp salt

½ cups shallots, chopped fine

Whisk together all ingredients.

OYSTERS ON THE HALF SHELL

Choose a type of oysters you enjoy, being sure to pick the freshest available (see sidebar). Open shells and remove oysters according to instructions (see sidebar). Serve on ice immediately after opening with a ramekin of Champagne Mignonette.

How to Open Oysters

1. At least an hour before you plan on opening them, scrub oysters under cold water. Ensure that each is closed tightly. If not, give it a slight squeeze. If it is still alive, it should close immediately and stay closed. If it doesn't, it is dead and should be thrown out.

2. Then oysters should be placed on a tray and put into refrigerator. You can even put them in the freezer, but only for about 10 minutes before opening. The cold relaxes them and makes them less resistant to opening.

3. Before you open them, check again for a tightly closed shell.

4. Place one oyster on a folded towel with the shell's flat side face up and its hinge side toward you.

5. Fold towel over top of oyster and press down firmly to hold it in place.

6. Choke up on oyster knife and insert tip into seam of hinge on shell.

7. Slowly insert knife and begin to twist it until the shell pops open.

8. Run knife along inside of top of oyster until you have cut the top muscle. Unhinge top part of the shell and remove it, making sure not to spill the oyster juice (liquor) inside.

9. Keeping shell upright and steady, run knife between oyster and bottom shell until you have cut the bottom muscle.

10. Place oyster on a flat bed of ice. This will preserve its flavor and keep it level.

Continue until you have opened and removed all of the oysters you plan to serve.

Rumson, where I grew up, is a small town at the northernmost tip of the New Jersey shore. It is bounded on the north by the Navesink River, on the south by the Shrewsbury River and on the east by the Atlantic Ocean. We lived about a mile in any direction from sea or river. When we drove just about anywhere, we would see fishermen crabbing or surf fishing. Commercial boats that took people out on the ocean to catch bluefish, striped bass or tuna were not uncommon.

When I worked at the Fromagerie, one of my coworkers, Nick Pietrone, was an avid fisher, and he invited me to go fishing off the Manasquan inlet. It probably wasn't the best idea, since I am highly prone to motion sickness and had never been out on the ocean. However, Nick convinced me to go, assuring me that we would be on a large boat and that it wouldn't rock as much as a small boat would. But I ended up being sick for 90 percent of the trip. I did catch a few fish nevertheless, and despite my sickness I came to understand why some people love to go fishing. The sudden tug of a bite just when you are giving

up makes fishing as tempting as playing golf in the hopes of hitting that one perfect ball. When the boat docked that day, we had about a hundred bluefish to clean. Nick began demonstrating how to do it and cut his hand with his filet knife. So I ended up cleaning and gutting about eighty fish. My hands stunk to high heaven, but I loved it!

Dungeness crab, named after the town of Dungeness in Washington State, is a sweet, large, meaty crab found on the West Coast and in the Pacific Northwest of the United States. They are in season during winter months. Like any crab, Dungeness crabs should be purchased live or precooked.

There are different approaches to eating a Dungeness crab. The shells of Dungeness are not as hard as those of Maryland crabs, but a nutcracker can be helpful. I like to save the meatiest part for last, so I start with the legs. The meat is so delicious that I don't mind working for it, so I don't skip any of the legs, regardless of size. Next, I attack the claws by pulling off the smaller joint to loosen the meat. Finally, I work on the main body of the crab. I take the triangle-shaped shell off the bottom and pull the top shell off. Then I hold the crab with two hands and firmly snap it in two. I remove the gills (and you can remove the "crab butter," if you don't eat that part). I snap the remaining two pieces in half again and enjoy the succulent meat at the top of the legs!

The finale and pièce de résistance for Thien on those fresh seafood nights was following up the extravagant first course with an equally large bowl of steamed Dungeness crabs seasoned with bay leaves, rosemary, thyme, garlic and shallots. Roberto, being from the Midwest, hadn't eaten a lot of shellfish before this tradition began, so at first we had to demonstrate how to eat them. Despite the fact that Roberto has impeccable table manners, it took him a few times to master the art of eating various types of seafood. But over time he, too, could eat Dungeness crab with great efficiency and tact!

Here is a recipe that is fun and delicious; it can be used for cooking live lobsters as well. The secret to keeping everything succulent and not overcooked is to bring the water to a boil, turn off the heat and keep the pot covered until the seafood cools.

steamed dungeness crabs with lemon

Serves 4

4 live Dungeness crabs

water

1 Spanish onion, halved

8 cloves garlic

1 sprig fresh rosemary

1 sprig fresh thyme

1 bunch fresh parsley

1 lemon, halved

salt

3 T Cajun seasoning

3 T olive oil

1 cup white wine

Place all ingredients in a large pot. Bring to a boil. Add crabs and boil for 12 to 15 minutes. Remove from water to cool. Serve immediately with a huge bowl for shells and shell-crackers for novices. Be sure to have plenty of napkins on hand!

wine of the people versus
wine of the kings

In addition to being an occasion for many wonderful meals and wines, Sunday night also became the battlefield for an ongoing competition between Roberto and Thien about which wine is superior—burgundy, wine of the kings, or bordeaux, wine of the people. This age-old debate was carried out on a weekly basis at Fork in the form of various wines, with each man trying to outdo the other with his selections.

Roberto first became fascinated by burgundy when he and his brother bicycled through the French countryside in the summer of 1993. As Roberto tells the story, they stopped at Drouhin Estates, unannounced and in their bicycle gear, looking like they had just finished a leg of the Tour de France. At first they were told that the estate—which houses an esteemed winery—could be toured by appointment only. But by coincidence the lovely Veronique Drouhin happened to walk by, and she volunteered to show them the cellars, despite the time of day and their unkempt appearance. After we opened Fork, Roberto mentioned to me several times that it would be great to invite Veronique for a dinner featuring Drouhin wines, all the while believing that she would surely remember him.

In May 2004 I saw that she would be in Philadelphia for a special wine dinner at Susanna Foo, a well-known local restaurant. I called Roberto and reserved a table for us. At the restaurant he and Thien immediately launched into a competition about which of the two would be able to get her to come to Fork. As they awaited her arrival at our table anxiously, they created various scenarios. But the one that came true hadn't been in their repertoire. Sadly for Roberto, Veronique didn't remember the

A green mango is an unripe mango. When making a recipe that calls for green mangos, choose the hardest mangos you can find and put them in the refrigerator to avoid additional ripening.

dashing, boyish young man who had been so impressed with her in his late twenties. However, fortunately for Thien, she does like Vietnamese food and was very happy to come to Fork for dinner the next night so she could enjoy some of Thien's cooking! Thien wanted to create a meal she would remember. The first course was a light start that featured seared sea scallops with a ginger-lime coulis.

pan-seared scallops with ginger-lime coulis aside cucumber green-mango slaw

Serves 4 as a dinner appetizer or light lunch

GINGER-LIME COULIS

¼ cup olive oil

1 T lime juice

3 T minced ginger

1 tsp honey

½ tsp fish sauce

salt and freshly ground black pepper to taste

Mix all ingredients together in a food processor or blender. Set aside.

CUCUMBER GREEN-MANGO SLAW

½ English cucumber, julienned

½ cup green mango, julienned thin using a Japanese mandoline

½ bunch Thai basil, chiffonade

½ red onion, sliced into half-moon shapes

2 T freshly squeezed lime juice

2 T rice-wine vinegar

2 T extra-virgin olive oil

salt and freshly ground black pepper

Mix all ingredients together when ready to serve.

PAN-SEARED SCALLOPS

12 jumbo dry sea scallops, or approximately 1¼ pounds

Kosher salt and freshly ground black pepper

1 T olive oil

Pat scallops dry and season with salt and pepper. Heat olive oil in a large sauté pan over medium-high heat until hot but not smoking. Sear scallops in pan, about 2 minutes on each side.

Place scallops on plates and drizzle with coulis. Place a mound of Cucumber Green-Mango Slaw to the side of each plate. Garnish with baby greens.

Culandro, **culantro** or sawtooth herb is similar to cilantro and is used in Southeast Asian cooking. It can be served fresh but is more often used to flavor dishes as they cook.

Vietnamese rice papers (galettes de riz) are thin, dried, round rice-paper wrappers made from white rice and tapioca powder. Just before use, rehydrate them by dipping them into warm water. Vietnamese rice papers are used traditionally to make spring rolls and summer rolls, the most well known of which are called *goi cuon*. They contain pork, shrimp, vermicelli and scallions. Vietnamese rice paper can accompany many traditional Vietnamese dishes, such as grilled grape leaves.

The sumptuous scallops were followed by a variation on one of my favorite classic Vietnamese dishes, grilled Vietnamese grape leaves with beef. Instead of beef, we wrapped a whole fresh fish with grape leaves before grilling it. Once the grape leaves have been grilled, they add a great charred taste to the fish. This dish sounds complicated, but it is one of the simplest Vietnamese preparations. It is served family style, so your guests will have to do some of the work. After the fish is grilled, each guest wraps pieces of fish in rehydrated Vietnamese rice paper with some Vietnamese rice vermicelli, fresh herbs, carrots and cucumbers. The wrap is similar to a spring roll and is dipped into your favorite sauce. This coconut-lime coulis is my favorite. Wrap as you go!

grilled red snapper in grape leaves with vietnamese rice-paper wraps and coconut-lime dipping sauce

Serves 4 as a dinner main course

COCONUT-LIME DIPPING SAUCE

½ can coconut milk

1 T fish sauce

½ jalapeño pepper, seeded and minced

1 T culandro (see sidebar), chiffonade

¼ cup lime juice

1 T rice-wine vinegar

Combine all ingredients and set aside until ready to serve. Place into individual ramekins or dipping bowls (one for each diner).

GRILLED RED SNAPPER IN GRAPE LEAVES

1 bunch fresh cilantro

1 bunch fresh mint

1 bunch fresh Thai basil

1 large carrot, peeled and julienned

1 cucumber, deseeded and julienned

1 package Vietnamese rice vermicelli, cooked according to instructions

red oak lettuce leaves

bibb lettuce leaves

one 7-pound whole red snapper, cleaned and scaled

1 jar grape leaves in brine, rinsed in water

1 lemon, sliced into thin rounds

4 to 6 sprigs fresh thyme

In a large serving bowl, assemble herbs, carrots, cucumber, lettuce and rice noodles. Allow space for grilled fish.

Preheat grill. Stuff stomach cavity of fish with lemon slices and thyme and season fish with salt and pepper. Wrap body of fish in grape leaves until surface of fish is completely covered. Brush hot grill grates generously with oil. Carefully place fish onto grill. Grill 8 minutes on one side and carefully turn. Grill an additional 8 minutes, or more if necessary. Place grilled fish in serving bowl with herbs and noodles. Serve family style.

RICE-PAPER WRAPS

1 package dried Vietnamese rice papers (galettes de riz)

1 bowl very hot water

To make a roll, dip a rice paper into a bowl of hot water. Quickly turn the paper so that entire surface comes in contact with water. It will start to soften quickly. Be careful not to leave it in the hot water for too long or it will tear. Place softened rice paper on a plate and arrange several small pieces of fish, herbs, vegetables, noodles and lettuce at one end of the roll. Roll it away from you once. Fold sides over and roll to the end of the paper. Serve with Coconut-Lime Dipping Sauce. After making the first one, you'll realize how easy this is!

Just when we thought we couldn't eat any more, Thien served a giant, herb-crusted rib eye. Veronique and her guests were excited, since in Europe it is unusual to get such a tasty "American" steak.

herb-crusted rib-eye steak

Serves 4 to 5 as a dinner main course

1 boneless rib-eye roast,
    4- to 5-pound

¼ cup Kosher salt

1 sprig fresh rosemary, leaves only

1 sprig fresh thyme, leaves only

1 cup fresh parsley leaves

½ fennel bulb, chopped into
    large pieces

5 garlic cloves

½ white onion, chopped

Preheat oven to 425°F. Combine rosemary, thyme, parsley, fennel, garlic and onion in a food processor and purée to a thick paste. Pack outside of meat, first with salt all around and then with herb crust on top. Transfer to a roasting pan with a flat rack.

Roast meat at 425°F for the first 15 minutes. Reduce heat to 375°F and continue roasting for 1 hour and 45 minutes or until a thermometer registers 125°F for medium rare. Remove meat from oven and let it stand for about 15 minutes before slicing. The internal temperature will continue to rise as it stands.

BON VOYAGE DINNER AND CUVÉE CHAMPAGNE

The competition between Roberto and Thien comes to a head during champagne season. For Thien, that season begins immediately after Thanksgiving and continues until New Year's. During this time, Thien's goal is to celebrate the holidays by enjoying at least one bottle of cuvée champagne per day.

Cuvée champagne is less common than other champagnes, though some types are rarer than others. Most cuvée is nonvintage—made from a blend of grapes from several years. In contrast, the grapes used to make a vintage cuvée are all from the same harvest year, a year when superior growing conditions have produced grapes of exceptional quality. Cuvée champagne is intended to represent a house's finest champagne. Sometimes it is vintage, sometimes not.

During this season, Thien can easily find an excuse to enjoy his champagne throughout the day or night, and various friends and staff may be invited to enjoy it with him. Every Sunday during these weeks, we start our meal with one of Thien's cuvée selections. Roberto, of course, being equally generous, brings in a bottle to share. By the time the new year arrived after our first champagne "test," the group's consensus was that Krug Grand Cuvée was the best. The only

thing better than a bottle of Krug Grand Cuvée, according to Roberto, would be a magnum, which Thien insisted would be impossible for Roberto to obtain. Saying this to Roberto was like throwing down the gauntlet. We knew he would seek to meet the challenge.

Every year in February, Thien needs to return to Switzerland and France to handle personal affairs. And travel by any member of Fork's core group gives everyone a legitimate excuse outside of the holiday period to have champagne and throw a bon-voyage dinner. Thien is always worried that one of our bon-voyage dinners might be the last time we will all see one another. At least, he says, we will have had a memorable meal together prior to the end! He gets especially worried about his own trips. We understand Thien's worry and always plan to have dinner together upon his return.

Two months after we decided that Krug was the best cuvée, Roberto diligently sought a magnum of Krug while Thien was away. Naturally, he was able to find it. Upon Thien's return from Europe, a magnum of Krug Grand Cuvée was waiting on the table when Thien came out to join us. Thien was beside himself!

pan-roasted duck with sauce chasseur, sautéed porcini and chanterelle mushrooms, baby bok choy and creamy polenta

Serves 4 as a dinner main course

SAUCE CHASSEUR

2 T olive oil

1 medium carrot, chopped

1 celery stalk, chopped

½ cup chopped shallots (about
    2 large shallots)

2 T brandy

8 to 10 fresh shiitake mushrooms,
    destemmed (reserve stems
    for sauce)

4 fresh oyster mushrooms,
    destemmed

2 fresh portobella mushrooms,
    chopped

¼ cup dried porcini mushrooms,
    rehydrated in ½ cup hot water,
    liquid reserved

1 bay leaf

1 sprig fresh thyme

2 parsley stems

1 cup white wine

1 quart chicken stock

1 to 2 T butter

Heat olive oil in a Dutch oven or small stockpot over medium-high heat. Add carrots, celery and shallots and sauté for about 5 minutes. Deglaze pot with brandy and let liquid reduce until it is almost gone. Add mushrooms and sauté about 5 minutes. Deglaze pot again with reserved porcini liquid and white wine and let mixture simmer over moderate heat for about 8 minutes. Add bay leaf, thyme, parsley stems and chicken stock. Bring to a boil and reduce heat. Simmer for 1 hour.

Strain sauce in a fine sieve. Put strained sauce in a large sauté pan over high heat and reduce to one third of its original volume. Remove from heat and stir in 1 to 2 tablespoons of butter. Keep sauce warm until ready to serve.

CREAMY POLENTA

1 cup polenta

3 cups milk

1 cup heavy cream

½ cup grated Parmigiano Reggiano

¼ cup grated Fontina cheese

salt and freshly ground black pepper
    to taste

Bring milk and cream to a boil in a large pot. Add polenta in a steady stream, whisking constantly, until mixture begins to thicken. Allow it to come to a boil again, then cover and reduce heat to low. Stir with a wooden spoon every few minutes for 30 minutes. Add cheeses and stir to incorporate. Season to taste. Cover and keep warm.

PAN-ROASTED DUCK

4 duck breasts

Kosher salt

freshly ground black pepper

Preheat oven to 450°F. Score skin sides of duck breasts, taking care not to cut through meat. Season each breast with salt and pepper. Place duck skin side down in a hot pan over high heat. Sear until skin is crisp, about 5 minutes. Turn breasts over and transfer to oven. Roast about 5 minutes for medium rare. Remove duck from pan and tent with foil until ready to serve. Leave pan intact for next recipe.

SAUTÉED PORCINI AND CHANTERELLE MUSHROOMS

1 cup porcini mushrooms

1 cup chanterelles

1 T duck fat (from roasting pan)

salt and freshly ground black pepper

Drain all but 1 tablespoon of duck fat from roasting pan. Return pan to stove over medium heat and add mushrooms. Sauté until they are just tender, about 5 minutes. Season to taste with salt and pepper. Set aside and keep warm.

BABY BOK CHOY

4 heads of baby bok choy, sliced in half

2 T olive oil

salt and freshly ground black pepper to taste

Add bok choy and olive oil to hot pan and sauté for 5 to 8 minutes, until vegetables are crisp-tender. Season with salt and pepper.

To assemble plates, cut and reheat polenta. Arrange polenta in center of plate, sprinkling grated Parmigiano if desired. Set duck breast on top of polenta. Place sautéed mushrooms and bok choy to side of duck and drizzle dish with Sauce chasseur.

The next dish was served at one of our most memorable bon-voyage dinners before Thien left for his annual trip home. The secret to this recipe is its full-bodied, collagen-rich chicken stock that simmers for hours, which is readily available to our cooks at the restaurant. At home, you can use store-bought chicken stock, though the end result won't have the same viscosity. Or you can make your own stock (see recipe in Fork Foundations). Either way, the dish will boast the earthy depth of chanterelle mushrooms.

Sauce chasseur (hunter's sauce) is a classic French brown sauce made from mushrooms, shallots and white wine. It is often served with game and other meats.

a special cuvée

From time to time, we hold special wine dinners. Initially, the dinners featured the wines and foods of a particular region, such as Piedmont in Italy, the Rhone Valley in France or Tuscany in Italy. However, as we progressed, the series began to feature specific wineries. Because of this shift in focus, a friend of Roberto's introduced us to a winery called Henriot Champagne. The staff had recently held a dinner at the prestigious Fifth Floor in San Francisco, so we knew that our dinner at Fork had to be special. A meal that would accompany five types of champagne, three of which were vintage, had to be over the top. Before 2004, Beluga caviar was not endangered, and we chose it for one of our dishes. Until that night, I hadn't appreciated what a match salty caviar and butter toasts are with champagne.

The winemaker, Stanislas Henriot, flew in from Paris only minutes before the dinner began. As a surprise, he brought one magnum each of 1990 and 1978 champagne. The menu was totally French and totally soignée!

Beluga Caviar with Buttery Toasts **NV Brut Souverain**

Day-Boat Sea Scallop Ceviche and Gigamoto Oysters on the Half Shell
NV Blanc de Blancs

Chicken Congêlée **Brut Vintage 1995**

Pan-Roasted Lobster over Fennel-Endive Salad with Passionfruit Vinaigrette
1988 Cuvée des Enchanteleurs

*Pan-Roasted Squab with Sauce Chasseur, Sautéed Chanterelles
and Mashed Purple Potatoes* **Rosé Brut 1996**

The Henriot champagne dinner affirmed me as an official Francophile. I was looking forward to my next trip to Paris. Little did I know that the inspiring ideas from my last trip would actually delay my ability to plan my next visit!

4

FORK NEXT DOOR

Our many stops at cafes, cheese shops and *traiteurs* (prepared-foods shops) form some of my fondest memories of our last trip to Paris. Looking back over those experiences confirmed my sense that good coffee, baked goods, prepared foods and wine make a perfect combination. I thought to myself that creating a new retail establishment that served these items might give Fork a new twist. I envisioned something really European—a place where one could get great artisanal products as well as prepared foods.

At that point, in 2002, Fork was running fairly smoothly; I could afford to take time for a vacation, to go out to dinner elsewhere or to spend a Saturday afternoon away from the restaurant. But I was getting antsy. In the past, I had been able to find projects to entertain myself. We had put out monthly newsletters, created wine dinners and other special dinners centered around authors, and found maintenance and renovation projects to pursue. But finally the urge to find another project became more and more intense. Perhaps this retail project could satiate that urge.

the seven-year itch

We had been approached with new opportunities fairly often in our seven years of operation, but none had come to fruition. Then, in 2002, the neighboring dollar store closed. I had never really considered the possibility that this space would become available, so I was caught off guard. At first I tried to rent the space, but the owner of the building and I were unable to reach an agreement at that time. So I sat by as projects such as an Indian restaurant and a movie lounge were proposed to the neighborhood zoning committee. With Old City burgeoning with nightclubs and bars, many of my customers urged me to rent the space to prevent undesirable concepts or even competition from affecting our investment.

Part of my lack of serious interest came from my concern about the effect that expansion would have on the current Fork, which was working very well already. While I was excited about the concept of a retail establishment that would sell prepared foods, I knew that the space was too large for a store. We had to figure out the right uses for the space.

That turned out not to be too difficult. Fork's main dining room is incredibly intimate but not ample enough for groups of ten or more. When we had opened, we anticipated that tables of two and four would be in highest demand. After only a few months, however, we found that the most common party size was six. In our early years, we could tell people that we didn't seat parties over ten. But as competition became more intense, we had to seat these larger groups. Yet it is far more difficult to prepare twelve hot dinners so that they are ready at the same time than it is to make two or four, especially in a small kitchen. Adding to this pressure to seat larger groups were the numerous calls we received each week from people interested in private dining. Clearly, a private dining room next door would be an asset to Fork.

So with the idea of a private dining room behind a retail establishment, we started developing a business plan for the new addition. By this time, Old City and Center City were experiencing a boom. Nearly every old industrial building in the neighborhood was being converted into million-dollar condominium complexes, and real-estate values were skyrocketing. Yet with so much new residential growth, Old City still had no supermarket or grocery store, in part because few properties in the area were large enough to hold one. Could the space adjacent to Fork fill that gap in neighborhood services?

In my mind, specialty grocers occupy a special niche. In my twenties, when I lived and worked in Rittenhouse Square, my favorite lunch-break activities were window-shopping at Bonwit Teller and buying a to-go lunch at the popular Frog Commissary on Seventeenth and Sansom Streets. The Frog Commissary was owned by Steve Poses, who also created a restaurant called Frog. I remember looking at all of the choices of healthy prepared foods, pastries and snacks at the commissary and not being able to decide what to eat. Philadelphians consider the Frog Commissary a landmark in the city's restaurant development, but it closed before Fork had even opened. Although the company remained open as a caterer, by 2002 nothing had really replaced the commissary.

As I discussed these thoughts with Roberto, we remembered one other wonderful thing about Paris: the bread, which was always fresh, delicious and easy to find. We envisioned walking on Third Street and smelling the aroma of fresh bread coming from our bakery. We saw a practical advantage to having our own bakery, as well; rather than buying it from a local artisanal bakery as we had since our opening, we could make it on site and thus ensure its total freshness and availability.

So we negotiated again with the landlord and came to an agreement. With the lease signed and Marguerite Rodgers on board to design the space, we embarked on a new journey that would bring many challenges, including the tasks of developing a new product mix, creating a new bakery and filling more seats. In summer 2004 we hired a baker to make artisanal bread using our own sourdough starter and bought a stone-hearth, steam-injected oven from Germany. And in November 2004, we opened Fork:etc, our gourmet prepared-foods cafe, which is open from 7 A.M. until 8 or 9 P.M., depending on the time of year.

The design and renovation of the space was a challenge, but determining what to sell and what not to sell was even more of a challenge. At the start, our primary offerings were coffee and pastries. But we found out quickly that our customers wanted breakfast, so we started serving omelets, an egg panini and waffles as well. Now that word has traveled, our regular crowd starts arriving as soon as we open so they can get our muffins and scones fresh out of the oven.

Here is our basic muffin recipe, which can be altered to include various fruits, nuts and spices. When you modify the recipe below, simply maintain the proportion of liquid to dry ingredients. For example, to use fresh berries instead of figs, substitute a half cup of berries for the half cup of figs listed. The orange zest can be omitted or exchanged for another flavor. For a chocolate-chip muffin, substitute chocolate for the fruit.

orange-fig muffins

Makes approximately 1 dozen muffins

1 cup granulated sugar

1 stick butter, room temperature

zest of 1 large orange (about 1 T)

2 eggs

1 cup milk

1 T orange juice

½ tsp vanilla extract

1½ cups all-purpose flour

1 tsp baking soda

1 tsp baking powder

½ tsp salt

½ cup dry figs, chopped

Preheat oven to 350°F. Grease and flour 12 muffin cups. Cream butter and sugar with a paddle attachment until they are light and fluffy. Add eggs and beat to incorporate. Add milk and vanilla, mixing to combine. Whisk together flour, baking soda, baking powder, salt and figs. Fold wet ingredients into dry ingredients until just combined. Place muffin cups into pan. Fill muffin cups two-thirds full. Transfer pan to oven and bake approximately 20 minutes, or until a toothpick inserted in the center of a muffin comes out clean.

Scones were always popular at brunch in the dining room. So we included them in our mix of daily baked goods at Fork:etc. Again, to alter the fillings, maintain the same proportion of dry and wet ingredients.

lemon-blueberry scones

Makes approximately 8 scones

2 cups all-purpose flour

½ cup granulated sugar

1 T baking powder

½ tsp salt

1 T lemon zest

1 stick plus 2 T unsalted butter

½ cup blueberries

2 eggs

½ cup heavy cream

Preheat oven to 350°F. Whisk flour, sugar, baking powder, salt and lemon zest together in a large bowl. Work butter into dry ingredients with your fingers to form a crumbly mixture. Gently stir in blueberries. Whisk eggs and heavy cream together. Stir wet ingredients into dry ingredients with a fork just enough to combine, taking care not to overmix. Gently push dough together into a ball and turn out on a floured surface. Pat it down into a 1-inch-thick round disk and cut it into 8 wedges. Transfer wedges to a cookie sheet lined with parchment paper or a Silpat. Bake scones until golden brown, about 20 minutes.

Our savory scones have a serious following. Nothing beats the aroma of these cheddar-cheese scones when they first come out of the oven. You can substitute any cheese or herb.

cheddar-chive scones

Makes approximately 8 scones

2 cups all-purpose flour

1 T baking powder

½ tsp salt

1 stick plus 2 T unsalted butter, very cold

¼ pound cheddar

1 T chives, chopped fine

1 T bacon (optional)

2 eggs, lightly beaten

½ cup heavy cream

Preheat oven to 350°F. Whisk flour, baking powder and salt together in a large bowl. Work butter and flour together with your fingers to form a crumbly mixture. Gently stir in cheese, chives and bacon. Whisk eggs and heavy cream together. Stir wet ingredients into dry ingredients with a fork just enough to combine, taking care not to overmix. Gently push dough into a ball and turn out on a floured surface. Pat it down into a 1-inch-thick round disk and cut it into 8 wedges. Transfer wedges to a cookie sheet lined with parchment paper or a Silpat. Bake scones until golden brown, about 20 minutes.

Since we were making our own brioche bread and challah, sticky buns were not much of a departure. And we knew they would be popular. After all, who can resist the sight of these big, gooey buns? You can add nuts or a fruit glaze on top.

brioche sticky buns

Makes 12 large or 24 medium muffins

1¼ cups warm water

4½ to 6 cups flour

⅓ cup sugar

4 eggs

1 stick (4 ounces) butter, room temperature, cut in pieces

2 T half and half

1 T fine salt

2 T plus 3/4 tsp yeast

2 T butter, melted

1 cup light brown sugar

1 T cinnamon

Combine water, 1 cup flour, sugar, eggs, half and half, and yeast in bowl of a mixer fitted with dough-hook attachment. Incorporate and let stand for 2 minutes. With mixer running, add remaining flour a little at a time. As dough starts to form, add butter pieces and salt. Knead dough for about 5 minutes, until a distinct ball forms. Turn dough out onto a floured surface and knead by hand an additional minute. Cover with a clean kitchen towel, put in a warm place and let dough double in size, which takes about 2 hours.

Punch dough down and press it into a rectangle of about 12 by 15 inches on a floured surface. Brush melted butter across dough rectangle, leaving a ½-inch border all the way around. Sprinkle brown sugar and cinnamon on top of melted butter. Starting with long side close to you, roll dough into a snug cylinder shape. End with seam-side down. Cut in 1-inch-thick rolls and place each roll into a greased jumbo muffin tin. Cover tin with a clean kitchen towel and allow dough to rise again, about 30 minutes. Preheat oven to 350°F. Transfer buns to oven and bake until they are golden brown and baked through (internal temperature on a thermometer should read 190°F), approximately 30 minutes. Let buns cool slightly in pan. Turn them out and serve warm.

Mirepoix is the basis of almost all French soups, stews and sauces. It is a mixture of herbs, carrots, onions and celery that have been chopped fine and sautéed in butter or olive oil. Ingredients vary but must include carrots, celery and onions.

Lunch was an immediate hit with the local businesspeople and residents. At lunchtime, the menu at Fork:etc focuses on sandwiches, soups and salads. Prepared foods can include simple items such as roast chicken, herbed pork loin, roasted potatoes, pasta salad, sautéed greens and other seasonal choices. Breads from our bakery include baguettes, multigrain loaves, brioche, focaccia and challah.

One of the biggest sellers at Fork:etc is soup, especially in the wintertime. A regular customer who is Swiss told me that whenever he goes to a new restaurant, he tests out the simplest dishes to see how well they are executed. Soup is always one of them. So I am glad that he likes our soups. This black-bean soup is vegetarian, but meat lovers can add a ham hock or chicken broth for additional flavor.

spicy black-bean soup with sour cream

Serves 4 to 6

1 pound dried black beans, soaked and cooked (see page 37)

¼ cup olive oil

2 stalks celery, diced small

1 large white onion, diced small

1 large carrot, diced small

2 green peppers, diced small

4 cloves garlic, minced

1 bay leaf

3 T chili powder

2 T ground cumin

1 T oregano

2 tsp ground coriander

12 cups water, vegetable stock or chicken stock

6 large plum tomatoes, diced

2 chipotle peppers, minced

2 T salt, or to taste

¼ cup chopped fresh cilantro

ham hock (optional)

Heat olive oil in a large saucepot over medium-high heat. Add celery, onion and carrot (mirepoix), green peppers, garlic and bay leaf. Sauté approximately 10 minutes, until vegetables are soft. Add dry spices and sauté 3 minutes to release flavors. Add cooked black beans and water. Bring to a simmer and cook 20 minutes. Add diced tomatoes and simmer another 10 to 20 minutes. Add chipotle peppers, salt and chopped cilantro. Remove bay leaf. Purée soup with an immersion blender in pot or in batches in a blender or food processor. Serve with sour cream and scallions.

In the wintertime, another favorite soup at Fork:etc is Thien's Tomato Beef Barley Soup. This soup is hearty, rich and filling.

tomato beef barley soup

Serves 4 to 6

1½ pounds chuck, cubed

2 T olive oil

1 cup carrot, chopped

2 celery stalks

2 cups onion

1 red bell pepper, cubed

1 T tomato paste

2 garlic cloves

one 16-ounce can plum tomatoes, crushed

2 star anise, crushed

4 cloves, crushed

1 bay leaf

12 cups beef stock

½ cup dried barley

salt and freshly ground black pepper to taste

Season chuck cubes with salt and freshly ground black pepper. Heat olive oil in a large saucepot or Dutch oven. When oil is hot, brown cubes on each side. Do this in batches to avoid steaming meat. Remove browned cubes and set them aside. Add carrots, celery, onion, bell peppers and tomato paste to pot. Stir to work up browned bits from bottom. Sauté vegetables for about 5 minutes. Add garlic and sauté an additional minute. Stir in tomatoes, star anise, cloves, bay leaf and stock. Simmer for 1 hour. Add barley and simmer an additional 30 minutes or until barley is done. Remove bay leaf. Season with salt and pepper to taste.

Fork:etc sells many items served in the restaurant, including dips and charcuterie. The Spinach-Artichoke Dip has been one of the most popular. You can spread it on sandwiches or serve it with crudités. Anne-Marie initiated the crispy pita chips. Since they don't keep long, they are best when eaten immediately after frying.

spinach-artichoke dip with crispy pita chips

Serves 4 to 6 as an appetizer

1 cup spinach, washed and destemmed

1 T extra-virgin olive oil

8 ounces cream cheese

one 14-ounce can artichoke hearts, drained

2 cloves garlic

1 T lemon juice

½ cup grated parmesan cheese

1½ tsp Kosher salt

¼ tsp freshly ground black pepper

Heat olive oil in a medium skillet over medium-high heat. Sauté spinach briefly, just until wilted. Place spinach, cream cheese, artichoke hearts, garlic, lemon juice, parmesan cheese and salt and pepper in a food processor. Blend mixture until it is smooth and all ingredients have been incorporated. Serve with Crispy Pita Chips and olives. Drizzle with olive oil to finish.

CRISPY PITA CHIPS

4 Greek pitas

2 cups canola oil

salt and freshly ground black pepper

Heat oil in a Dutch oven or large pot until it registers 365°F on a deep-fry thermometer. Cut each pita into 8 triangles. Working in batches to avoid overcrowding, carefully drop pita pieces into hot oil and fry until golden. Scoop pita out with a slotted spoon or spider, or with tongs. Transfer to a cooling rack lined with paper towels to drain excess oil. Season with salt and pepper.

This dip was developed by one of our sous chefs, Ali Cobbett. Thien enjoys teaching, and over the years he has trained aspiring chefs of all levels in the kitchen. Thien always has the hope that one of them will take his job and allow him to retire! Many have worked for a year and then sought a new experience. But Ali was an exception: she was Thien's grandest experiment. Could he take someone with no experience who was highly educated and had good values and a strong work ethic and turn her into a chef? For a year, Thien taught her his recipes and trained her himself. By the end of the year, she was running the kitchen as sous chef.

Tzatziki is a Greek sauce or dip made from strained yogurt, cucumbers, onion, sometimes garlic and fresh herbs. Tzatziki is often served with pita and olives.

tzatziki

Serves 8 to 10 as an appetizer

1 pound plain, lowfat yogurt or 1½ cups thick Greek yogurt

½ English cucumber, halved lengthwise, seeded and diced into ¼-inch pieces to yield ½ cup

½ cup red onion (or more to taste), chopped fine

¼ cup fresh mint (any type), chopped fine

1 clove garlic, minced and mashed with coarse salt to form a paste

½ tsp Kosher salt

freshly ground black pepper to taste

Place yogurt in cheesecloth-lined strainer set over a bowl. Refrigerate for at least 2 hours to drain. (You can eliminate this step if using Greek yogurt, which is already very thick.) After yogurt has drained, fold in cucumber, onion, mint, garlic, salt and pepper. Adjust seasoning to taste if necessary.

At Fork, we always use **free-range chickens** because they have been treated more humanely and are healthier and more flavorful. Free-range chicken is not the same as organic chicken, and organic chicken is not necessarily free range. Free-range chickens are leaner because they are allowed to roam and forage and live in natural light. The term organic, when applied to chicken, indicates that the chicken has eaten only organic feed.

In Paris I was fascinated to see chickens being roasted in rotisseries right on the sidewalk, with a dozen or so chickens turning on each rotisserie and a big pan of roasted potatoes sitting on the bottom. I decided right then that roast chicken was a must for Fork:etc, but unfortunately we don't have the space for a large rotisserie. Instead, we roast chickens fresh daily and place them in our display case. Customers still love the recipe, even though the display is not nearly as interesting as a rotisserie.

herb-roasted, free-range chicken

Serves 2 to 4 as an entrée

one 3-pound free-range chicken

4 T butter

1 sprig fresh thyme

1 sprig fresh rosemary

2 cloves garlic

1 shallot

Kosher salt and freshly ground
    black pepper

butcher string

Preheat oven to 375°F. Rinse chicken and dry off inside and outside with a paper towel. Season inside cavity. Stuff inside of chicken with 2 T butter, thyme, rosemary, garlic and shallot. Truss chicken by tying drumsticks together. Liberally season outside of chicken with salt and pepper. Place 2 T of butter on top of chicken. Place chicken in a roasting pan. Roast for approximately 1 hour, or until skin pulls away from drumstick. Allow to sit 15 minutes before serving.

Roast chicken always tastes better with its natural accompaniment, roasted potatoes. We chose fingerling potatoes, which are small, thin potatoes that resemble a finger in size and shape.

roasted fingerling potatoes

Serves 4 to 6 as a side

1 sprig thyme

1 sprig rosemary

1 bay leaf

2 cloves garlic, peeled

1 shallot, peeled

4 T Kosher salt

cold water

2 pounds unpeeled fingerling
    potatoes

2 T olive oil

freshly ground black pepper

Preheat oven to 400°F. Place herbs, bay leaf, garlic, shallot, salt and potatoes in a large pot. Fill pot with water to cover potatoes. Bring water to a boil. Remove from heat. Allow potatoes to sit in water 20 minutes or until water is cool enough to touch. Pour into a large colander to drain water. Cut fingerling potatoes into halves. (Smaller potatoes may be left whole if desired.) In a large ovenproof skillet or pan, heat olive oil. Add potatoes and pepper. Stir to coat potatoes with olive oil and pepper Place skillet or pan in the oven and roast for 8 to 10 minutes.

Since we serve coffee and cappuccino, dessert is always in high demand at Fork:etc. This flourless chocolate cake is rich and delicious. It doesn't last long.

flourless chocolate cake

Makes one 9-inch cake

1 pound bittersweet chocolate, cut into small chunks

2½ sticks (10 ounces) butter

½ cup sugar

7 eggs

Preheat oven to 350°F. Cover bottom of a 9-inch cake pan with parchment paper and grease entire surface. Fill bottom of double boiler halfway with water. Combine chocolate and butter in top half and put double boiler over medium heat. Melt chocolate and butter slowly, stirring regularly with a rubber spatula or wooden spoon to avoid scorching bottom. While chocolate and butter melt, whip eggs and sugar together in bowl of a mixer fitted with whisk attachment. Beat until light, fluffy and nearly tripled in volume. When chocolate is completely melted and smooth, pour it into eggs in a slow, steady stream with mixer running on low speed. Pour batter into cake pan and set cake pan into a baking dish or roasting pan. Transfer to oven and pour enough hot water into dish so it comes halfway up sides of cake pan. Cover cake pan with foil. Bake for approximately 1 hour, removing foil halfway through. Cake is done when a fork inserted in its center comes out nearly clean, with a few crumbs. Remove cake from oven and allow to cool slightly. Carefully invert cake onto a cooling rack and remove parchment paper. Cool completely before cutting. A berry sauce complements this cake well. Serve with whipped cream, if desired.

holiday catering

Everyone told me that the way to make Fork:etc succeed financially was to get into catering. Since you know just how many people you're serving and what dishes to make, there's no waste, and catering an event doesn't involve the operational headaches that the restaurant does. So we thought we'd try it out. We began by catering for three Jewish holidays (Rosh Hashanah, Yom Kippur and Passover). In order to satisfy a broad range of dietary traditions, we stuck with a few basics, such as roasted chicken, braised brisket and braised lamb. And of course, since we now had a European-style bread bakery, we made matzoh by hand for Passover and challah for the fall holidays, though we don't run a Kosher kitchen.

We soon learned that you can't make just roasted chicken and braised brisket and expect people to want to order meals for their family. So we expanded the menu to include chopped liver, gefilte fish and kugel. When we planned to introduce these additional items I explained to Thien that chopped liver was like a chicken-liver pâté and that gefilte fish is like quenelles or Asian fish balls with added matzoh. But my explanations were insufficient in some cases. At first, I got exactly what I had asked for—Asian fish balls masquerading as gefilte fish. I tried to explain to Thien that these were traditional foods and might not be the best outlets for creative interpretation. But most chefs don't follow recipes, and Thien is no exception. Nevertheless, the next time Passover rolled around, I handed Thien the *New York Times Jewish Cookbook*. That, too, raised complications: when someone ordered potato kugel, he followed the recipe for stove-top potato kugel and made them in the form of potato latkes—not what the customer had had in mind. Over time, however, our offerings have come a bit closer to the expected. This recipe for seared chicken livers is popular year round.

pan-seared, five-spice-dusted chicken livers aside spinach salad with caramelized onions and lemon vinaigrette

Serves 4 as a lunch entrée or 6 as an appetizer

CARAMELIZED ONIONS

½ red onion, sliced thin

1 tsp olive oil

salt and freshly ground black pepper
    to taste

Heat oil until it is medium hot.
Add sliced onions and sauté over
medium heat until they are soft
and translucent. Add salt and pepper.
Continue to cook until onions are
caramelized (an additional 5 to
7 minutes). Put aside and cool to
room temperature.

LEMON VINAIGRETTE

2 tsp lemon juice

½ tsp honey

2 T extra-virgin olive oil

salt and freshly ground black pepper
    to taste

Whisk ingredients together.

PAN-SEARED, FIVE-SPICE-DUSTED CHICKEN LIVERS

1 pound chicken livers

2 T ground five-spice powder

8 T all-purpose flour

1 T olive oil

2 T marsala wine

½ pound baby spinach, cleaned

1 T lemon juice

salt and freshly ground black pepper

In a bowl, combine five-spice powder
and flour. Season livers with salt
and pepper. Then dust livers with
seasoned flour.

Heat pan on high. Add olive oil.
When pan is hot, add livers. Sear
for 2 minutes on each side until
livers are crispy. Add marsala, cook
30 seconds and remove from heat.
If using a gas stove, marsala may flame.
Turn off heat when flame dissipates.

Lightly dress spinach with dressing.
Create a bed of baby spinach on
a plate and place livers on top. Add
caramelized red onions to salad.

Caramelizing onions, shallots
or garlic releases their natural
sweetness. To caramelize, melt
butter, olive oil or bacon fat in
a pan over medium heat. Add
chopped or sliced onions, shallots
or garlic. Reduce heat to medium
low and cook them slowly until
they are soft and golden brown
but not burned. (Garlic tastes
bitter when burned.) Stir frequently,
scraping sides and bottom of pan
to incorporate fat and juices.

Brisket is usually a tough cut of meat, but this recipe transforms it into a tender, flavorful dish.

beef brisket braised in red wine

Serves 6 to 8 as a dinner main course

3 pounds beef brisket, trimmed

1 tsp whole black peppercorns

¼ cup olive oil

4 cloves garlic

1 Spanish onion, chopped

5 carrots, peeled and cut into 1- to 1½-inch pieces

5 stalks celery, cleaned and cut into 1- to 1½-inch pieces

1 small fennel bulb, chopped

½ cup parsnips, peeled and quartered

1 bay leaf

1 sprig fresh rosemary

1 sprig fresh thyme

½ cup tomato purée

1 cup red wine or port

1 to 2 quarts meat stock or beef broth (see recipe in Fork Foundations or use store-bought)

Preheat oven to 350°F. Season brisket with salt and pepper. In a Dutch oven, heat oil over high heat. Add peppercorns. Sear brisket until browned. Remove brisket from pot. Set aside.

Over high heat using same oil, add garlic and onions. When onions become caramelized, add carrots, celery, fennel and parsnips. Continue stirring until vegetables are browned, about 5 minutes. Deglaze pan with red wine or port. Put brisket back into pan. Cover with meat stock. Add tomato purée, bay leaf, thyme and rosemary. Place in oven and cook approximately 3 to 3½ hours, until tender.

Because we have our own bakery, Fork's kitchen has a constant supply of day-old bread for bread pudding. Day-old bread is ideal for this recipe.

white-chocolate cherry brioche bread pudding

Makes one 13-by-9-inch pan

1 loaf brioche or challah (about 24 ounces), cut into 1-inch cubes

6 eggs, lightly beaten

4 cups cream

1 cup sugar

½ tsp salt

1 T vanilla

1 T almond liqueur or almond extract

1 cup white chocolate chips or chunks

1 cup dried cherries

Preheat oven to 350°F. Grease a 13-by 9-inch baking dish. Put bread cubes in dish. In a bowl, whisk together cream, sugar, salt, vanilla and almond liqueur or extract.

Pour liquid mixture evenly over bread cubes.

Sprinkle chocolate and cherries on top and gently press down on bread cubes. Cover and let soak for at least 15 minutes. Transfer to oven and bake, uncovered, for 45 minutes to 1 hour, until custard has set.

chef's bistro dinner

No one but Meg Rodgers could have designed our expansion into the space next door. Her task was to make the space feel continuous with the restaurant but unique. Its private dining room was relatively simple; it had to be elegant and accommodate parties of varying sizes without seeming too big or too small. Fork:etc was more of a challenge. I had mixed thoughts about how the space should look. On the one hand, I felt that Fork:etc should be warm and welcoming. But on the other hand, I wanted it to be modern and contemporary. I also wanted it to be related to Fork in some way. Meg came up with the perfect solution: she put in a tile floor that looks similar to the concrete bar she designed for Fork, and she replicated the Maine-farmhouse windows used in Fork's entry.

Meg thought Fork:etc should be more than a gourmet store; she felt that it, too, should be suitable for use as a private dining venue after the store closed. In the center of the room, she envisioned a big table where everyone could sit together. Thien loved the idea and thought it could be used in ways that resembled one of his favorite places in Paris. As he tells it, on his way home from work, he would stop at a restaurant called Madame Muscatere, where local chefs went to eat after work. It was a very small place, almost a hole in the wall. Every night, Madame Muscatère would cook whatever she felt like cooking, usually lots of stews and braised meat. When you were done eating, you'd get up and the next person in line would sit and eat, until the food ran out and she closed for the night. Thien thought that creating his own Madame Muscatère in the center of Fork:etc on Wednesday nights would be an enjoyable way to express his creativity. As he saw it, these Wednesday nights could offer him a way to experiment with the menu, a spinoff of the Sunday-night dinner but for paying guests! Soon after we opened, we put the plan into action. The only times our Wednesday-night dinner is cancelled are when Thien is sick or out of the country!

No doubt in part because of the relative novelty of the concept, Wednesday nights at Fork:etc took a while to take off, even though the inexpensive price (forty dollars including wine) was attractive. The dinner is first come, first served and begins at 8 P.M. Although our guests wanted reservations, I refused to take them because I wanted Thien to have his desired freedom of expression regarding the menu. If I took reservations, people would call and say, "I'm coming, but I don't eat mushrooms." Naturally we go out of our way to accommodate food allergies, but for Wednesday-night dinners at Fork:etc, we aren't able to alter the dishes

served. Still, people can find out in advance whether a particular meal will work for them. Every week we post the menu on the restaurant's website and on the chalkboard at the entrance of Fork:etc.

In any case, at first the turnout was small. The usual suspects were me, Wayne, Chris Curtin (a friend of Roberto's who is a master chocolatier and owner of Éclat Chocolates), Kevin Hills (our florist) and one or two other people. Occasionally Thien would make an appearance.

A SAUSAGE CELEBRATION

On one of the first Wednesdays, we met a couple celebrating their anniversary. Dinner that night featured sausage as the main ingredient of every course. Retired and in their late sixties, the couple decided to celebrate at Fork:etc because the husband loved sausage. Although that dinner was not well attended, it gave us the opportunity to get to know these folks. The story of how they met was memorable: both the husband and his brother had been Fulbright scholars in Europe, he in London and his brother in Rome. He was burned out from studying and needed a break, so he went to Rome. When he arrived—and keep in mind this was in the 1950's—he told his brother that he really wanted to go out on a date. Nothing serious, he just wanted some female companionship, dinner and good conversation. A young Swedish woman had just moved into the same apartment building as the brother, and the brother thought that she might be open to meeting new friends. So the brothers and a few friends stopped by her apartment to see if they could coax her into going out with them. They hollered up to the window until she appeared. She was tired and not really in the mood to go out, but eventually they convinced her. That night, the couple got to know each other, and they spent a lot of time together over the next week.

Then he headed back to London to return to school. Soon after, he received a letter from her that said she had had a wonderful time with him and was planning to head back to Paris and then to Sweden. She thanked him for a lovely week and wrote that, by the way, she thought she loved him. Upon reading this, he immediately rushed out to send a telegram that said that he also had feelings for her and that she should stay put because he was on his way. He rushed back to Rome and sent for all of his books. Several months later they were married. They celebrated their fiftieth wedding anniversary with sausages.

SEAFOOD SAUSAGE WITH CUCUMBER SALSA

VEGETARIAN SAUSAGE WITH SALAD GREENS

DUCK SAUSAGE WITH PEAR COMPOTE

PORK SAUSAGE WITH GUACAMOLE AND CHIPS

MINT SORBET

5

As much as I love France, I'm at least equally enamored with Italy.
Thanks to Roberto, who is first-generation Italian American and
speaks impeccable Italian, I have visited Italy many more times than
I have visited France. Since 1998, we have traveled there at least ten
times together. On our first trip, we visited what once had been his
grandmother's vacation home in Liguria, on the Italian Riviera.
The memories of his childhood brought up by that visit prompted him
to plan at least one vacation a year in Italy. But these were not long
sojourns; in the early stages of Fork, getting away for more than five
days in a row was virtually impossible. As a result, we would leave on
a Wednesday night and return on a Sunday night. Despite the briefness
of those visits, I was able to relax completely. No one at home believed
that this was possible when I told them, but it was true: as soon as I got
in the taxi to go to the airport, Fork became very far away. And once we
were there, of course, that feeling deepened. Sitting on a beach of stones
and looking out onto the Mediterranean, with a small medieval town
behind me and a friendly bar a few steps away, it was easy to let go
of my other life.

On most evenings, we ate at one of the restaurants that Roberto had researched. At the time, I spoke no Italian, so Roberto had to translate every menu. I found it hard to choose, as everything sounded great and looked great. Since our eyes were always too big for our stomachs, we would bring leftovers back to the house. Roberto taught me to make them into frittata the next morning for brunch or lunch.

piedmont

The two or three times we visited Liguria, we made a side trip to Piedmont, where the famous Italian wines Barolo and Barbaresco are made. Naturally, these trips had to include some sort of a wine tasting or tour. Our first visit was to the estate of Roberto Ferraris, whose Barbera d'Asti had been extremely successful at Fork. For the first time I experienced real Italian hospitality. Many people had told me that Italians are very generous when it comes to entertaining. I knew about such generosity from my own childhood, when I would often sit at dinner with my aunt, who was raised in Japan. Regardless of how much I had eaten already, she would keep scooping more food onto my plate. However, Italian hospitality brought this phenomenon to an even higher level. I love Italian food, so when Mrs. Ferraris brought out antipasto, I ate it. Whatever she brought out, I ate. And the more I raved about the food and ate, the more food she brought out! After becoming completely full, we drove to our next stop in Serralunga d'Alba to see Stephano Bruni of Cascina Bruni. Roberto had helped out in the orchards there a few years earlier, during the harvest. There, we only had to drink some of his magnificent 1995 Barolo. We skipped dinner.

The next year, we drove directly from Nice to Piedmont, where we planned to eat at Da Cesare in Albaretto della Torre. I felt as though we had landed in the middle of nowhere. Cesare himself greeted us when we stepped into his bed and breakfast across the road from the restaurant before our meal. (After such good food and wine, no one should have to drive.) His property sat on the edge of a hill, overlooking a gorgeous view of a valley filled with perfectly manicured grape vines. We came upon him at around 6 P.M., just in time to enjoy the sunset and a glass of wine with Cesare. You'd think a restaurant in such a remote area would not be busy, but we had to beg to be squeezed in at 8, the equivalent of 5:30 in Philadelphia. The restaurant was completely filled with locals by 9:30.

Overlooking the valley at the Roberto Ferraris winery in Asti, Piedmont, with the Ferraris family

That night we learned what amazing food Piedmont had to offer. A wood-burning fireplace with a rotisserie greeted us as we entered the restaurant. Roast pork and lamb were slowly turning and cooking on the open fire. One dish on the menu included fresh porcini mushrooms sautéed with peaches; another was a smoked pheasant salad. But naturally the pièce de résistance was the spit-roasted meat. When we were ready for the meat course, the server brought over a large platter of assorted cuts and asked which piece or pieces we wanted. Later in the meal, when we were thoroughly stuffed, she brought the dish over again and asked if we wanted seconds! The meal ended with fresh strawberries tossed in balsamic vinegar, the perfect ending to a great meal. At that point, we were all starting to feel the effects of travel and were happy to roll over to Cesare's bed and breakfast.

Although I had had strawberries marinated in balsamic before, the dish reminded me that almost any summer fruit can be served in the same way. Upon our return, we added Figs in Balsamic to our dessert menu; however, Thien added a twist by heating the figs with the balsamic, which gave a sweet, syrupy flavor to the dish.

figs sautéed in balsamic with vanilla gelato

Serves 4

1 pint fresh black mission figs,
  washed and halved

1 tsp olive oil

¼ cup granulated sugar

¼ cup balsamic vinegar

1 pint vanilla gelato or ice cream

Heat pan over high heat. Add olive oil. Toss figs in oil. Add sugar and balsamic. Stir and continue heating until balsamic is reduced. Serve immediately over ice cream.

The next morning we started off at 9 A.M. with a visit to Stephano's estate, which began with another tasting of his most recent Barolo. Stephano and his sister lived together, but sadly his sister could no longer walk due to multiple sclerosis. Both times we visited, Stephano carried his sister into the living room so she could enjoy conversation with us. Even though I didn't understand most of what they were saying, I could sense how much they enjoyed hearing about Roberto's life in the United States and his perceptions of current events. When we left after our second visit, Stephano referred us to a wine store in Alba, which we visited. The store's owner recommended a restaurant called La Libera for lunch, and that lunch turned out to be one of my most memorable meals in Italy, especially because of the cheese plate we were served. Cheese was a specialty of the house. At the entrance of the restaurant stood a huge wooden block with about twenty different perfectly aged and ripened cheeses on it, all made from unpasteurized, raw milk from the area. The cheese plate we ordered had a huge impact on both Roberto and me.

As a child, I feared cheese; it was a very foreign ingredient, not used in Chinese cooking. I still remember when my younger brother's friend brought Borden cheese squares to our house when I was in the third grade. They were little wrapped cubes, only about a half-inch square. On first glance, I thought they were caramels, so I popped one in my mouth. The shock of tasting an unexpected processed cheese caused me to spit it out immediately! But even if I hadn't been expecting a candy, the unfamiliar smell and milky taste of the cheese were food characteristics to which I wasn't accustomed. Even pizza or grilled cheese were unthinkable for me at that time; when those items were on the lunch menu at school, I brought my lunch.

My dad, however, loved cheese, even stinky blue cheese. He had acquired this taste while living by himself when he first moved to the United States. When we were teenagers, he convinced us all, including my grandmother, to try pizza. Eventually, pizza became a part of our weekend routine. My guess is that we outgrew our picky-eating stage—although to this day my mom does not eat cheese.

Soon after I began working at the Fromagerie, I had no choice but to confront my cheese phobia. (Ironically, "fromagerie" means "cheese dairy.") At lunch, the restaurant served quiche, fettuccine Alfredo and fondue, all of which exuded strong cheese aromas. This was, after all, the 1980's! After seeing so many of these dishes go out, I thought to myself that perhaps I was missing something. When I tried them, I found that they weren't as bad as I had expected them to be.

La Terrasse, the French restaurant I worked at, served cheese at the bar, including camembert, the creamy, mushroomy, soft-ripened cheese; Boursin, the commercial, herb-flavored cream cheese; and edam, the yellowish Dutch cheese with a wax rind. None of these were too challenging for me to eat; in fact, I found them tasty enough for a bar snack with a French baguette. Often, when the camembert was ultraripe, we bartenders would finish it off with Carr's wafers at the end of the night.

When we first opened Fork, I had remembered how much I enjoyed having a glass of wine and cheese at La Terrasse. I thought that we should at least offer cheese on the dessert menu, so we did. At that time, our cheese plate was extremely simplistic, offering only domestic brie, goat cheese and Gorgonzola or Cotswald cheddar. One afternoon several years later, a member of our kitchen staff was setting up a cheese tray before sending it out the door as a donation to a charitable event. When I saw that the person was piling up cubes of provolone and Swiss, I immediately instructed him to stop. Cubes of provolone and Swiss are available through any basic caterer. I knew that whatever we sent to the event would create an image of Fork in the minds of those who ate it. At that moment I realized that I needed to learn more about cheese, because I wanted to make a change.

When I returned from our trip to Piedmont, I was doubly determined to revamp the cheese menu. One day I stopped at the Reading Terminal Market, one of Philadelphia's largest farmer's markets, and tried out a few cheeses at

Downtown Cheese. The owner, Jack Morgan, is extremely knowledgeable—so knowledgeable, in fact, that cooks from area restaurants sometimes work behind his counter to learn about cheese. I asked Jack to help me find a few varieties suitable for our cheese plate. We started out with five, and the number grew quickly to ten.

Once we had revamped the cheese plate, I thought it would be a great idea to promote it by inviting an expert to the restaurant. I noticed that a new book had come out called *The Cheese Plate* by Max McCalman, *fromager* of Picholine Restaurant on the Upper West Side of Manhattan. I remembered Roberto telling me that Picholine was known for having one of the best cheese offerings in the country. Max's book describes how he became interested in cheese and offers some basics on cheesemaking, but I was particularly interested in his thoughts on pairing wines with cheeses. Though by then my knowledge of cheese had increased, the only way I knew to pair wines with cheeses was by geography.

So we invited Max to our first cheese dinner in September 2002. Max was a character. He arrived with a suitcase full of cheese from Artisanal, a restaurant formed by Terrance Brennan, the chef at Picholine, that focuses on cheese and has a wholesale business. The remaining cheese was to come from Downtown Cheese, so we took a cab there to inspect the cheeses for our dinner. Max picked up a wheel of Époisses, a pungent French washed-rind cheese that truly defines stinky when it is ripe. He brought it to his nose and inhaled the aromas. I loved his passion and his dedication to cheese.

At that first dinner, we offered three cheese plates of four cheeses each, plus a light supper preceding them. By the dessert course, we were all cheesed out! The wine pairings were fairly traditional. We started by selecting some cheese-friendly wines: a bright, citrusy New Zealand sauvignon blanc; an Italian Langhe wine made from Nebbiolo grapes, the same varietal used to make Barbaresco and Barolo; and a French Jurançon, a sweet, raisiny dessert wine.

SEPTEMBER 2002 CHEESE DINNER WITH MAX McCALMAN

KOURA BAY, SAUVIGNON BLANC, 2001, NEW ZEALAND

Selles-sur-Cher (Goat, Loire Valley, France)—Ashed rind; sweet, nutty flavor

Brin d'Amour (Sheep, Corsica, France)—Dried and herb coated; herbs are edible but bitter

Los Beyos (Goat, Spain)—Lightly smoked cheese

Ossau-Iraty (Sheep, Pyrenées, France)—Nutty, olive-like, fruity flavor; inedible brushed rind

FONTANAFREDDA, "COSTE RUBIN," BARBARESCO, NEBBIOLO, 1997, ITALY

Ibores (Goat, Spain)—Hard, dense, rubbed with olive oil and sweet paprika

Taleggio (Cow, Piedmont, Italy)—Washed rind with rough, reddish-brown rind; meaty, nutty, salty flavor; stinky

Piave (Cow, Friuli, Italy)—Hard, truffly cheese

Vacherin Fribourgeois (Cow, Switzerland)— Grassy and nutty, with an aroma of hay

JURANÇON, PETIT MANSENG, 1997, FRANCE

Époisses (Cow, Burgundy, France)—Soft, washed red rind, stinky cheese

Roncal (Sheep, Navarra, Spain)—Hard, three-month aged, rich, olivey, nutty

Farm Gouda (Cow, Netherlands)—Rich, sharp, three-year-aged, complex, nutty

Peral (Cow, Asturia, Spain)—Creamy blue

Some of these cheeses were added to Fork's cheese menu immediately, and eventually some also became standards at Fork:etc, our gourmet store. And I learned some simple lessons from this dinner. First, I learned that strong cheeses, particularly blue cheese, pungent washed-rind cheeses or aged cheeses, complement dessert wines particularly well, because the sweetness and acidity of the wine offset the saltiness of the cheese. I learned, too, that lighter, more delicate cheeses can go well with a crisp white instead of a red. Most importantly, I learned that pairing a wine with a cheese is a complex task that is partly a process of trial and error.

Fortunately, one can get assistance from experts such as Max. Over the years, Max has maintained a database of the notes he has made while tasting cheeses from all over the world and the wines that accompanied them. These notes formed the basis for his most recent book, *Cheese: A Connoisseur's Guide to the World's Best*, for which he received a James Beard Foundation Award. Even as Max gives talks and attends dinners and book signings, he manages to stop by Fork at least once a year.

collelungo

By 2000, Roberto decided that he had had enough of renting places in Italy: he wanted his own place. Liguria is a tough place to visit for long weekend trips, because you have to fly first from Philadelphia to London and then on to Nice, with no room for delays. On one trip we nearly missed our connection, but Roberto somehow convinced a British Airways representative to whisk us from Terminal One to Terminal Four beneath the bowels of Heathrow Airport so we could catch our connecting flight. I felt as though I was in an action movie! To avoid such stresses, Roberto decided that one criteria he would use in choosing a property was that it could be reached via a direct flight from Philadelphia. He began looking in southern Tuscany, which is only an hour-and-a-half drive from Rome. By 2001, he had discovered and acquired Collelungo, a ruin twenty minutes from Montepulciano and Montalcino that needed serious renovation. Roberto was impressed by the beautiful countryside and the tranquility of the surrounding area.

Aerial view of Collelungo

On our first visit to Collelungo, we discovered how much easier it was to get there than it had been to get to our earlier destination. Since the house was under construction, we stayed in a small bed and breakfast close by. As usual, Roberto had done his research and found all the great restaurants in the area. However, we found it terribly exhausting to eat every meal in a restaurant for more than five days straight. Generally, every meal began with an assortment of delicious Tuscan salamis and cheeses, followed by pasta, meat and, of course, wine. When Roberto's contractor told us about the community truffle festival in the nearby town of San Giovanni d'Asso, we were excited to get a break from our routine.

As we were in a very remote area of Tuscany, we hadn't imagined that a small-town festival could be so crowded, but it was; we couldn't even find parking nearby. Finally, we parked and met up with Roberto's contractor, who directed us to a party in the basement of a local bar. Admission couldn't have been more than fifteen dollars a person. The dinner included the usual assortment of Tuscan cold cuts and cheese, pasta with truffles and grilled sausage, but it was less formal than our restaurant meals had been; we felt as though we were at a family barbecue. There was a grill set up for meat and bruschetta. The bruschetta, toasted with the local olive oil and sea salt, were so simple yet so tasty. They were toasted just enough to have a nice crunch to them.

I thought about whether we could pull off such a fresh and simple item at the restaurant. Sometimes, the simpler the dish, the harder it is to make consistently well on a large scale. But we tried it on our return, and our version has become a staple at every Fork cocktail reception. You can also make bruschetta in a more rustic style, as Anne-Marie did with the Beet, Leek and Gorgonzola Bruschetta on page 38.

bruschetta with wild mushrooms and roasted garlic

Makes approximately twenty-four ½-inch bruschetta

1 head of garlic, roasted
(see page 18)

12 ounces mixed wild mushrooms
(such as portabella, shiitake,
crimini and oyster)

1 shallot, minced

2 T olive oil

½ tsp salt

freshly ground black pepper

1 bunch fresh parsley leaves, minced

baguette or artisanal country bread,
sliced in ½-inch diagonals,
brushed with olive oil

Preheat oven to 350°F. Dice mushrooms into small pieces and toss with olive oil, salt and pepper. Spread mushrooms out across a baking sheet lined with foil. Roast mushrooms in oven for 15 minutes.

Place bread slices on a baking sheet and toast on second rack of oven for about 5 minutes. Toss roasted mushrooms with minced parsley. Spread roasted garlic paste on toasted bread slices and top with about 1 tablespoon roasted mushrooms.

Bruschetta originated in Central Italy, where Italians have long grilled bread and rubbed the toasts with garlic, olive oil, salt and pepper. Traditional bruschetta are often topped with roasted peppers, tomatoes, vegetables, cheese or prosciutto.

bistecca

In 1993, when I had just graduated from business school, I traveled to Florence and had the famous bistecca Fiorentina. Perhaps we just didn't order it from the right restaurant, because it didn't leave a lasting impression on me. Or perhaps the meat wasn't authentic; true bistecca Fiorentina is made from the large Chianina oxen that graze in the Val Di Chiana in southern Tuscany, close to Collelungo. Even though I hadn't been impressed, however, I was willing to try it again. But the first few years I visited Collelungo, bistecca was difficult to find because of the outbreak of mad cow disease. However, by 2004, bistecca had started to reappear.

By this time, we had our travel routine down. We would fly into Rome, down two cappuccinos in the Rome airport, run to the Hertz terminal to rent a car and drive to Tuscany in time for lunch. Usually we hadn't eaten in ten hours or so and were a little tired from the trip, so lunch was the perfect time to get some red meat. If the weather was sunny and warm, Castelmuzio, with its great outdoor cafe, was our favorite spot. If it was rainy or cold, Forcillo, a rustic little family restaurant in Sinalunga, was a great alternative.

At Forcillo, the bistecca caught my attention. The steak was at least three inches thick, grilled with the perfect amount of caramelization and served with simple wedges of lemon and, of course, local olive oil. Steak is generally sold by the kilo in Italy and is often not cheap, especially after Italy's conversion to the Euro. So rather than buying the steak at Forcillo, I started investigating the area's food shops so that we could make our own. I found the shop of Macelleria Ricci, a local butcher in Trequanda, close to Collelungo. Besides offering very high-quality meats, fowl and cheese, this butcher shop is famous for its Chianina beef.

But we didn't seem to be able to get there on a day when they had any of the beef left. We went several times, and each time we were told that they were sold out of Chianina bistecca. Finally, Luca, the caretaker of Collelungo, told us the secret: we couldn't just order the Chianina steak; we had to order other cuts along with it. Because Chianina steak was in such high demand, this strategy enabled the butcher to offer it at a more reasonable price. So the next time we went in, we ordered pork chops and sausage in addition to the bistecca. Sure enough, they had it!

Back home at Fork, we hosted a wine dinner for Paolo de Marchi from the Isole e Olena estate in Chianti. Isole e Olena's Cepparello, named after a brook on Paolo's estate, is one of Roberto's favorite wines. We have offered every vintage since the award-winning 1997 wine put Isole on the map. Paolo is recognized as one of the best winemakers in the world, so it was a tremendous honor to have him at the restaurant. For such an important winemaker and wine, something special was in order. At most of our wine dinners, we have tried to prepare authentic food from the region from which the wine was derived. So at Paolo's dinner, we served a variation of bistecca Fiorentina using porterhouse steak. Chianina beef raised in the United States was difficult to track down and too expensive, so we used porterhouse.

At home, try dry, aged porterhouse steak that is at least two inches thick. Porterhouse steak has buttery filet mignon on one side and flavorful strip loin on the other. The secret to grilling it properly and attaining even caramelizing is to use a hot grill. Although at Fork we serve it in individual portions, in Italy we order one to one-and-a-half kilos (2.2 to 3.3 pounds), which arrives at the table on a platter and gets shared family style. You could certainly serve it this way!

grilled porterhouse steak with baby arugula salad, white beans, fennel and shaved parmigiano reggiano

Serves 4

Awaiting bistecca, Wayne, Gavin Argyle and Roberto

GRILLED PORTERHOUSE STEAK

4 porterhouse steaks, approximately 12 ounces each, cut a minimum of 1 inch thick, or 3 pounds of porterhouse steak, cut 2 inches thick

salt and freshly ground black pepper

extra-virgin olive oil

lemon slices

Heat grill. Grill meat approximately 5 to 6 minutes on first side. When steak can be easily turned, turn it. Cook other side for approximately 4½ to 5 minutes for medium rare, depending on thickness. Do not flip again. Move steak on grill if filet part cooks faster than strip steak. Season with salt and pepper after meat is cooked. Drizzle with olive oil. Garnish with sliced lemons.

SALAD

3 T freshly squeezed lemon juice

½ cup extra-virgin olive oil

pinch Kosher salt

8 ounces baby arugula

1 cup cooked white beans

½ fennel bulb, shaved

¼ cup shaved Parmigiano Reggiano

Whisk together lemon juice, olive oil and a pinch of salt. Toss arugula, white beans and shaved fennel with dressing in a bowl. Sprinkle shaved Parmigiano on top. Serve aside steak.

Usually our Italian sojourns occur in the summertime, when tomatoes and basil are at their best, so *insalata caprese* often precedes the bistecca. This salad must be made with unrefrigerated, vine-ripened tomatoes that are not too soft. The cheese should be bufala mozzarella or a good-quality, fresh cow's mozzarella *(fior di latte)*. Fresh basil picked straight from the garden, local olive oil, salt and pepper make this simple dish irresistible. Typically, Italians do not use vinegar on this salad.

At Fork, we are fortunate to get fresh tomatoes and basil from Branch Creek Farm. The farm's heirloom tomatoes vary in size, color and shape, so to take advantage of these tomatoes, Thien has created a few variations on the insalata caprese. At Fork:etc we use grape and pear tomatoes with *fior di latte ciligene* (cherry-sized cow's milk mozzarella balls) to make this simple salad. It could be served alongside a sandwich or fish or on a plate of greens.

tomato, mozzarella and cucumber salad

Serves 6 to 8 as a side salad

1 quart mixed cherry, grape, pear and/or pixie tomatoes (multicolored, if possible)

2 cups fresh mozzarella (ciligene, if possible)

1 English cucumber, seeded and sliced

½ cup extra-virgin olive oil

3 T white-wine vinegar

salt and freshly ground black pepper to taste

Cut larger tomatoes in half. Combine all ingredients in a bowl and season with salt and pepper to taste.

A more sophisticated twist on the salad uses peaches or avocado instead of mozzarella. But if you are a purist, you can stick with mozzarella! This Carrot-Ginger Vinaigrette is one of my favorite dressings.

Chiffonade refers to the fine ribbons obtained when several leaves of vegetables or herbs are stacked, rolled tightly into a cigar and cut into $1/16$- or $1/8$-inch shreds.

heirloom tomatoes, peaches and red onion with carrot-ginger vinaigrette

Serves 4 to 6 as a first course or light lunch

CARROT-GINGER VINAIGRETTE

½ pound carrots, chopped

3-inch chunk of ginger, peeled and cut into chunks

1 garlic clove, roughly chopped

1 tsp chopped shallot

2 T lime juice

2 T rice-wine vinegar

½ cup olive oil

½ tsp sugar

1 tsp salt

Purée all ingredients in a food processor. Strain through a fine-mesh strainer. Set aside.

SALAD

4 large heirloom tomatoes, cut into wedges

1 pint grape tomatoes, washed

1 pint pixie tomatoes, washed

4 ripe peaches, quartered

12 basil leaves, chiffonade

½ red onion, sliced thin

Place 2 tablespoons of dressing on each plate. Arrange tomatoes, peaches and onion over dressing. Sprinkle with chopped basil. Garnish with baby basil or other microgreens.

la cena cinese

By 2003, Roberto's house in Italy was finally ready to receive guests, and Wayne and I were lucky enough to be invited. Through the course of the two-year restoration, we had met some of the locals, including Roberto's general contractor, Azzolino; the stonemason, Paolo; the municipal-plan reviewer, Claudio, and his wife at the time, Sandra; Roberto's caretaker, Luca; and Luca's girlfriend at the time, Tiziana. So of course we wanted to have a dinner party. The house is perfect for dinner parties because of the long wooden table in the dining room that seats about fifteen. During that first visit and many of our subsequent ones, Roberto has invited the entire group over for dinner.

The seating arrangements at dinner always have to be planned so that conversation will flow. Luca, who can speak a little bit of English, is always seated near Wayne and me. The Italian-speaking-only group is gathered near Roberto. Sometimes these arrangements remind me of sitting with company when I was a child, when my parents might have been speaking in a dialect besides Mandarin or talking about something I didn't care to know. Wayne speaks some Italian, and the men at the table love speaking with him because his name reminds them of John Wayne.

Our dinner conversations range from politics to food. I discovered that they all loved Chinese food, but when they described what they liked to eat, I realized that it was definitely not authentic. So during our first dinner party I promised to make them Chinese food on our next trip. Roberto's is a great house in which to be a guest and an even better house in which to be cooking. The kitchen is a real kitchen, not a vacation-house one, with a gas stove and grill, a dishwasher, a large refrigerator, chef knives and a wood-burning pizza oven.

The next year, as I planned the dinner while in the United States, I wasn't sure what ingredients would be available in Italy. So I planned to bring sesame oil, rice noodles and soy sauce. But unfortunately we forgot the sesame oil and soy sauce. I went searching for them in Tuscany and was fascinated by the Co-op, the Tuscan supermarket chain. I enjoy shopping for food when abroad, especially when I get hints of how other people live by seeing what they can buy on a daily basis. I scoured several stores for sesame oil and soy sauce, and finally I found soy sauce—the kind in the little bottle with the red spout that's open on both sides, which you often see in Chinese restaurants. I also found ginger and spring onions, which were my saviors; otherwise, the food could not have been called Chinese!

Based on available ingredients, I came up with a menu that included one of my brother Mark's favorite dishes to make, Hainan Chicken. I took Roberto's pasta pot and put a cleaned, raw chicken in it. I filled it half with wine, half with chicken broth until the chicken was submerged. I added a half an onion, a bunch of spring onions and two inches of ginger chopped into four pieces. The pot was brought to a boil, and then I turned it off and let it sit. When it was cool, I pulled out the chicken and chopped it into pieces so everyone could share.

I also made sautéed chicken and fava beans, and after the dinner, Roberto kept asking me how to make it. I was pleased that he had liked it so much. When I was a child, my father's favorite dish was braised fava beans. The beans were removed from the pods and slowly cooked with garlic and olive oil until the beans were very tender. I don't know what I didn't like about fava beans then, but now I love them. In Italy, you often need not only to take the favas out of the pods but also to slip them out of their jackets, which makes fava beans a really high-maintenance dish.

To make my dish, I removed the fava beans from their pods, then blanched the beans in boiling water to remove their jackets. Meanwhile, I sautéed minced garlic, ginger and julienned chicken breast, which I had tossed with egg white, salt and pepper. Then I added chopped scallions and fava beans and seasoned them with salt and pepper. Because I love fava beans, I have often begged Thien to make something with them. This dish is Thien's solution to shelling fava beans: use edamame (soybeans) instead!

Prosciutto di Parma is a cured ham from the Parma region of Italy. Prosciutto di Parma is slightly nutty in flavor because the pigs it comes from are required to be fed the whey produced during the making of Parmigiano Reggiano. Prosciutto di Parma is known for its sweetness and tenderness, and true varieties are made without artificial preservatives. To maximize its flavor, Prosciutto di Parma should be sliced as thin as possible. The term Prosciutto di Parma is legally protected.

prosciutto di parma with edamame, fresh radishes, walnuts, parmigiano reggiano and citrus vinaigrette

Serves 4 to 6 as a dinner first course

CITRUS VINAIGRETTE

3 T lemon juice

¼ cup extra-virgin olive oil

1 tsp Kosher salt

Whisk ingredients together.

PROSCIUTTO DI PARMA WITH EDAMAME, FRESH RADISHES, WALNUTS AND PARMIGIANO REGGIANO

1 cup fresh or thawed frozen edamame (soybeans)

3 radishes, sliced thin and chopped

2 T grated Parmigiano Reggiano

½ cup walnuts, toasted

¼ pound prosciutto di Parma, sliced very thin

shaved Parmigiano Reggiano for garnish

extra-virgin olive oil for drizzling

Toss together edamame, radishes, cheese and vinaigrette. Top with toasted walnuts and shaved cheese. Drape prosciutto slices on plate around salad. Drizzle with extra-virgin olive oil.

the countess, the chef,
the author

Sometimes Fork wine dinners are organized around a well-known region, and sometimes they feature a winemaker. In the case of Anna Tasca Lanza, we had the luxury of having as our guest not only a representative of her family's wines but also a native chef and author.

We were able to invite this esteemed guest with the help of one of our customers. In October 1998, Fork was featured in *Wine Spectator* in a story by John Mariani. About a month after the issue came out, a guest told the staff to let me know that he was featured in the same issue. His name is Ed Bergman, and he is a wine collector and a Wharton professor. A few years later, Ed telephoned to let me know that he had arranged a wine dinner on behalf of Fork! He had just returned with his then-girlfriend and now wife, Jennifer, from Sicily, where they had visited the renowned Regaleali Estate. They met Marchesa Anna Tasca Lanza, whose father acquired the winery in the mid-1950's and whose family has run the winery since. Anna also operates a cooking school at Casa Vecchie on the estate's property, where she is essentially an ambassador for Sicily. Ed told me that Anna wanted to come to Fork for a wine dinner and asked if I would host her. Of course!

I was excited to use Fork's seasonal food concept and to introduce our guests to Sicilian cooking through someone with such authentic qualifications. However, when we started discussing dates, my heart sank. Anna was only available in February. What about the fava beans, artichoke hearts, blood oranges and wild fennel? Italian cooking is the epitome of seasonal cuisine, and I had dreamed of her coming in late spring or summer, when Sicilian ingredients could really be highlighted. However, this was not possible. So be it.

Not only was her first visit to Philadelphia in the winter, but when
Anna arrived in February 2003, there was more than a foot of snow.
Anna phoned me from her hotel room in New York City the night
before the storm. "If I can make it from Palermo to New York," she said
optimistically, "there certainly won't be any problem from New York
to Philadelphia." The following morning she called to tell me she was
snowed in and that there wasn't a taxi to be found on Seventh Avenue.

By the next morning, however, Seventh Avenue had finally been plowed. We greeted her later that day at Thirtieth Street Station in Philadelphia, snow boots and all!

I had scoured Anna's books to create an interesting menu for the cold weather. Major problem: *The Flavors of Sicily*, her second English-language book, described only what Sicilians ate from March through October. Then I found her recipe for roast baby lamb. Thien grew excited by the concept of cooking a whole animal. He found a whole baby lamb and hung it to air dry in the basement, shocking the many members of our staff who are vegetarians. But Anna had no such compunctions; she held the neck of the lamb, showing complete confidence in Thien as he brought the cleaver down and chopped off a piece of carcass. Since most people don't have access to whole baby lamb, we adapted this recipe from *The Flavors of Sicily* for use by home cooks.

agnello al vino (roasted lamb with red wine)

Serves 6 to 8

3 pounds lamb shoulder, cut into
   3½-inch pieces

salt and freshly ground black pepper

2 T olive oil

1 tsp whole black peppercorns

2 cloves garlic, chopped

1 red onion, coarsely chopped

1 carrot, chopped fine

1 celery stalk, chopped fine

1 fennel bulb, chopped

2 T tomato paste

2 to 3 sprigs fresh rosemary

2 to 3 sprigs fresh thyme

1 bay leaf

2 cups dry red wine

2 cups meat stock or beef broth
   (see recipe in Fork Foundations
   or use store-bought)

Preheat oven to 350°F. Season lamb well with salt and pepper. Heat olive oil in a Dutch oven. Add peppercorns and lamb, working in batches to brown meat on all sides. Remove meat. Add garlic, onions, carrot, celery and fennel to pan and stir until caramelized. Deglaze with 1 cup of red wine. Return lamb to Dutch oven. Add rosemary and thyme. Cover with meat stock.

Transfer to oven and roast about 1½ hours, until meat is tender. Take Dutch oven out and remove lamb. Keep warm. Place remaining roasting liquid on burner and add remaining 1 cup of red wine. Reduce over high heat, scraping bottom of pan. Season with salt and pepper. Pour sauce over lamb to serve. Roasted Fingerling Potatoes (see recipe on page 151) would be a nice accompaniment to this dish.

Deglazing a pan is an important stage in making sauce or gravy. The method uses a liquid—usually wine, stock or water—to collect the flavorful brown bits, or fonds, that remain in the pan after browning, sautéing or roasting. The resulting liquid usually serves as the basis for another sauce. To deglaze, remove excess fat left in pan (but not fonds). Return pan to medium heat, add a small amount of liquid and scrape bottom of pan with a wooden spoon to lift fonds. Add additional liquid as necessary.

One of the antipasti to which Anna introduced us is a Sicilian street food. *Arancine* are saffron risotto balls that resemble a small orange (called *arancia* in Italian) in shape, size and color. Since the dinner with Anna, arancine has been a staple on the Fork tapas menu and appears frequently at Fork:etc. The original recipe in *Herbs and Wild Greens from the Sicilian Countryside* can be a bit challenging, so we have simplified it.

Panko is a Japanese breadcrumb with a lighter, airier texture than its American counterpart. Tan-colored panko is made from the whole bread loaf, white panko from all but the crust. Panko breadcrumbs are great for making crusts or fried food because they grow crisp and turn a golden-brown color.

fork arancine (saffron rice balls)

Makes approximately thirty-two 1-inch arancine

STUFFING

10 ounces prosciutto di Parma
   or bacon, diced

¼ cup Parmigiano Reggiano
   or pecorino

RISOTTO

1 small onion, diced small

1 clove garlic, minced

2 T olive oil

1 pound risotto (arborio) rice

1 cup dry white wine

4 cups water

4 threads saffron

2 heaping T grated parmesan

1½ tsp Kosher salt

freshly ground black pepper

BREADING

2 cups panko (see sidebar)

2 quarts vegetable oil, for frying

Sauté prosciutto or bacon until it is crispy. Allow to cool. Mix with cheese. Set aside.

For risotto, sauté onion and garlic in olive oil in a large sauté pan over medium-high heat. Add rice and cook 5 minutes, stirring occasionally. Add wine and stir about 30 seconds. Add water and put lid on. As soon as liquid comes to a boil, add saffron. Stir again, let liquid return to a boil, replace lid and turn off heat. Let rice sit, covered, for 25 minutes. Stir in parmesan, salt and pepper. Pour risotto onto a cookie sheet lined with plastic wrap or aluminum foil. Spread out with a spatula and wait for it to cool.

Place panko on a shallow plate and set aside. Place a heaping tablespoon of rice in palm of your hand, cup it and push to create a little well in middle of rice pile. Fill well with ½ teaspoon stuffing. Close your hand over rice to enclose meat and form a ball. Add more risotto if needed. Place arancine in breadcrumbs and roll to cover. Set aside.

Heat oil in a deep pot or Dutch oven until it registers 360°F on a deep-fry thermometer. Pick up arancine in a slotted spoon and carefully roll it into oil. Fry in batches to avoid overcrowding oil. Turn balls in oil until they are golden brown. Remove from oil and drain on paper towels. Eat them while they are still warm.

Although artichokes are available year round, their prime growing season is from March to May. In Italy, where you can see them growing wild, the green of their leaves is often tinged with a deep purple, which gives the young artichokes a beautiful appearance. With Anna, we simply roasted them in olive oil. Our variation is braised with white wine, lemons, olives and mint. I love the flavor of the braising liquid, which tastes wonderful on pasta. Usually at the restaurant we serve the artichoke with the braising liquid in a bowl, accompanied by grilled bread and olive oil.

braised artichokes with white wine, mint and kalamata olives

Serves 6 to 8

6 to 8 large artichokes or
    12 to 18 baby artichokes

2 garlic cloves, peeled

2 shallots, peeled

1 bay leaf

1 sprig fresh thyme

1 sprig fresh rosemary

1 sprig mint

1 sprig flat-leaf parsley

½ cup Kalamata olives

2 lemons, halved

¼ tsp red-pepper flakes

Kosher salt to taste

2 cups dry white wine

½ cup olive oil

water

Preheat oven to 400°F. Clean artichokes, pull off tough outer leaves and cut off top third. Cut off stem so artichoke stands upright. Arrange in a large casserole or baking dish.

Add all ingredients to the casserole or dish. Add water if artichokes are not submerged in liquid. Cover with aluminum foil. Bake until artichokes are tender, about 1 hour and 10 minutes. Serve with braising liquid and grilled bread if desired.

a marchesa's seasonal garden

In May 2004, I made the long journey from Philadelphia to see Anna in Sicily. Valle Lunga is not an easy place to reach. It requires taking planes, trains and automobiles. When we finally arrived at the train station in Valle Lunga eighteen hours after leaving Philadelphia, Anna was waiting for us in her elegant country apparel. We stayed at her home, Casa Vecchie, on the Regaleali Estate. As we toured the estate and winery, Anna explained that her grandfather's wish was to be able to stand at any point on the estate and see only Regaleali. The property did seem endless.

The highlight of the visit was seeing Anna's magnificent garden, which was part flower, part vegetable. Her garden epitomizes seasonal cooking. During her classes, she brings groups out to her garden to select fresh vegetables for cooking. For our breakfast, we had fresh blood oranges from her tree. Another fruit we enjoyed from her garden was fresh loquats, which—as we quickly learned—mark anything they touch with their indelible juice. We didn't learn this quickly enough to save Anna's linen napkins. Sorry, Anna.

After lunch, Anna drove us through the countryside to Mondello, a waterfront town just outside Palermo, where she has a beach home. Watching Anna maneuver her Punto through the hills and valleys of Sicily on a stick shift was enough of a sight. However, the drive was also one of the most scenic I'd taken in Italy. It was spring, so the mountains were still green, and poppies spotted the fields. As we drove into Mondello, it seemed that everything, including outdoor sculptures, windows and streets, was adorned in pink and black. We later learned that these were the colors of Palermo's soccer team and that the towns were celebrating the team's advancement to the next league.

Because we were near the beach, the seafood in Mondello was amazing. The octopus salad in olive oil and lemon juice was so fresh. We also loved the fresh sardines with herbed breadcrumbs. Thien often prepares this dish at Fork during the short sardine season. The trick to this recipe is to sauté the breadcrumbs and herbs in olive oil until they are crispy. We make breadcrumbs from our day-old, housemade bread. You can use Italian breadsticks or flatbreads instead, if you prefer, and pulverize them in a food processor.

Segmenting an orange or grapefruit means removing all the skin, pith and membrane to free the juiciest part of the fruit. To segment the fruit, cut the ends off. Place the flat side of the fruit on a cutting board. Using a sharp knife, cutting downwards in curved strips, remove the skin and as much of the white pith as possible. Then, place the fruit in the palm of your hand. Using your knife, make a cut to the right side of the first segment, being careful not to slice the membrane. Repeat on the left side. Carefully loosen the segment and remove from the orange or grapefruit. Continue until all the segments have been removed.

grilled sardines with herbed bread crumbs aside baby arugula salad and orange segments

Serves 4

8 fresh sardines, scaled, gutted and head removed

olive oil for pan

2 T extra-virgin olive oil

1 T fresh rosemary, chopped fine

1 T fresh thyme, chopped fine

1 T fresh flat-leaf parsley, chopped fine

1 cup fine breadcrumbs

salt and freshly ground black pepper to taste

1 lemon, cut into wedges

2 cups baby arugula

4 T lemon vinaigrette (see page 154) or dressing of your choice

2 small seedless oranges, segmented (see sidebar)

In a frying pan, heat oil. When hot, add breadcrumbs and herbs. Continue stirring until breadcrumbs become crispy. Season with salt and pepper. Place herbs on a flat plate.

Heat grill. Brush sardines generously with olive oil. When grill is hot, place sardines on grill. Do not turn until fish can be loosened from grill, approximately 3 minutes. Turn to cook other side. When both sides are cooked, remove from grill.

Toss arugula and orange segments in desired dressing. Place each sardine on plate that contains breadcrumbs and generously cover sardine on both sides. Place sardines beside salad on a fresh plate. Garnish with lemon wedges.

pizza

A few years ago, Luca, the caretaker at Collelungo, introduced us to
a new pizzeria called Paradiso in Trequanda, right near Roberto's house.
Paradiso was owned by Luca's childhood friend Giorgio Perinti. His
wood-burning oven is made entirely out of bricks, so the walls absorb
the warmth of the burning wood and generate consistent heat even after
the fire has dissipated. This type of oven produces crispy, thin-crust pizza
that is absolutely delicious.

We got there at about 8:30 P.M., before the locals had started arriving.
By midnight, the entire parking lot, which acted as the outdoor cafe,
was full of people coming in for pizza, gelati made by Giorgio's mother
and other snacks. The energy surrounding Paradiso reminded me of
the atmosphere at Fork. I watched the customers interacting with Luca,
Giorgio and the other staff for hours; even though I couldn't understand
a lot of what was being said, I really felt at home. The staff were moving
efficiently, as well as greeting customers and seeming truly happy to take
care of them. The guests were enjoying themselves and interacting with
people at other tables. There was definitely a buzz. Our visit there was
one of the highlights of that vacation.

Experiencing the pizza at Paradiso made our friends want to try making pizza in the wood-burning oven at Collelungo. Luca showed us how to light it, and we proceeded to make ten to fifteen different types of thin-crust pizza in Roberto's oven. We thought we had mastered the technique, but we learned when Giorgio came to dinner that using this type of oven is an art.

Giorgio had brought some dough and tomato sauce from the restaurant, and Wayne had prepared the wood-burning oven according to Luca's instructions. But when Giorgio looked in, he shook his head and took over. We learned a few tips: no olive oil on the dough before baking, and no mozzarella cheese until the absolute last minute of baking. Giorgio started making pizza Marguerita, which he believes is the only authentic pizza, but then he relented and allowed everyone to build their own pizzas. He said in his charming Italian accent that Americans like too many things on their pizza. Excuse me! On his menu, there are twenty varieties of pizza!

We returned to Philadelphia inspired to create our own interpretation of pizza, using our stone-hearth bread oven. Although our dough is not as thin and light as Giorgio's, the pizza we sell at Fork:etc is tremendously popular. It is usually topped with our homemade sauce, fresh mozzarella and a few simple toppings, such as spinach, caramelized onions, fennel, shiitake mushrooms or olives.

the perfect panini

One of our rituals upon leaving Tuscany via Rome is to enjoy a panino and a beer at Tazza d'Oro, a restaurant that sits in front of the U.S. Airways gate. Even at the airport, these sandwiches are tasty. Usually they contain ham or salami sliced thin, and sometimes cheese and arugula, all of which is sandwiched in a thin piece of focaccia or ciabatta. At Fork:etc, we offer several grilled sandwiches. One of the most popular panini contains grilled eggplant, portobella, fresh mozzarella, arugula and pesto. When you make panini, don't push down on the press. The weight of the grill will automatically compress the sandwich.

grilled eggplant, portobella and mozzarella panini with basil pesto and fresh arugula

Serves 4

BASIL PESTO

1 bunch fresh basil

1 cup extra-virgin olive oil

¼ cup toasted pine nuts

¼ cup Parmigiano Reggiano

salt and freshly ground black pepper

Place ingredients in a food processor and purée. Set aside. Any remaining pesto can be refrigerated for up to a week.

GRILLED EGGPLANT, PORTOBELLA AND MOZZARELLA PANINI

1 eggplant, sliced and grilled

4 portobella mushrooms, cleaned and grilled

2 to 3 balls fresh mozzarella

1 cup baby arugula, cleaned

Basil Pesto

4 focaccia or ciabatta

Spread pesto on both halves of sandwich bread. Place eggplant, mushroom, mozzarella and arugula on bottom half. Cover with top half. Press in a panini grill or place in a hot frying pan with a teaspoon of olive oil and press with a heavy pan on top while panini cooks.

the best olive oil in the world

Each time we return to Collelungo, we see the property becoming lusher and more settled. Everything feels familiar when we turn onto the driveway and approach the house. The driveway, which is about a quarter-mile long, is lined with olive trees, some old and some more recently planted. Most Italians who have olive trees on their property use the olives to make oil. They take their olives to the local *frantoio*, or olive-pressing mill. Naturally Roberto began trying to make use of the olives on his estate by learning to make olive oil.

Italians are very parochial. They take pride in all products from their native region, and the people of each area believe that their products are the best. For example, when we told Anna Tasca Lanza that Roberto had started dabbling in olive oil in Tuscany, she immediately gave us a bottle of her estate oil so we could taste the true excellence of Sicilian olive oil, which she believed to be superior. And when we visited Roberto's uncle in Liguria, we found that the Ligurians felt that their olive oil was the best. There are definite differences between the oils. Ligurian olive oil is more buttery. Tuscan olive oil has that peppery green flavor that sometimes bites you in the back of the throat. And Sicilian oil is a little smoother but sometimes still tastes a bit green. Naturally, the differences are due to different olive varietals, as well as to *terroir* (those special geographic qualities that give foods their unique properties).

At first Roberto had brought his olive oil to the States in large containers and divvied it up among friends. Once he had begun trying to make olive oil in earnest, I was curious to get a closer look. So in November 2003, I accompanied him to Italy to help him pick olives. The November weather was crisp and cool. In the sun, it was sweater weather, so being outside for much of the day was fairly comfortable. To pick olives, we draped burlap around one tree at a time and shook the tree to get the

olives to fall. Then we stripped the olives off of individual branches with our hands. After they fell to the burlap, we inspected each olive carefully, discarded damaged ones and removed the stems and leaves from all the rest. I suppose it was tedious, hard work, but it didn't feel that way to me because it was such a great change from my day-to-day routine at Fork!

The trip was rewarding in another important way as well, because 2003 was the first vintage of Olio d'Oliva di Podere Collelungo to be packaged in a beautiful green bottle with an attractive label, and we were going to carry those first few cases on the plane home. But our flight was delayed eight hours, so we checked the oil and took the train to the neighborhood of Trastevere for lunch. The weather in Rome was a spectacular 70 degrees, an Indian-summer day. In the spirit of celebrating olive oil, I enjoyed one of my favorite Italian pasta dishes, Pici con Cacio é Pepé. The pici, which is rolled, long spaghetti similar to bucatini, is tossed with olive oil, local cheese (Pecorino Romano, in the case of Rome), salt and pepper. That afternoon, as we basked in the sun at the outdoor cafe, I decided to spend more time in Rome. As for the olive oil, we managed to get those first bottles on board the plane and back to the restaurant. When Fork:etc finally opened, we had plenty of Roberto's 2003 stock on our shelves.

making friends in rome

As it turns out, my Rome connection was not far from my home. One of my favorite restaurants in Philadelphia is a small BYOB in Rittenhouse Square called Melograno, which is owned by the chef and his wife, Luca and Rose DeMontis. Luca's family owns a restaurant in Rome, and Luca grew up in that city, so he knows Rome inside and out. Upon my return from olive picking, I asked them to suggest restaurants in Rome. They recommended a place called La Cassetta with great enthusiasm, but they warned me that it was off the beaten path, not in the downtown area. I shrugged my shoulders because I knew that wherever Luca and Rose sent us would be a tremendous place.

Before my next trip to Italy, I called La Cassetta to make reservations and spoke with Luca's childhood friend Massimo, the son of the owners. I realized that the family did not speak much English but made the reservation anyway. (Roberto would not be with us on this leg of the trip, so we wouldn't have him to translate for us.) When we arrived at the hotel in Rome, I tried to find the restaurant on the map. However, as La Cassetta was on the outskirts of town, it didn't appear on any of the tourist maps we had. Since Luca DeMontis had told me that it was near Piazza Bologna, we told our taxi drivers that the restaurant was in that area. Because we were a group of five, we had to take two taxis. I was in the cab that arrived at the restaurant first. We waited patiently for the rest of our party to arrive. But it was taking them unusually long. Suddenly the restaurant's phone rang and the hostess yelled out, "Chi parla inglese?" I knew that the call had to be for us, as we were the only English-speaking guests in the place. It turned out that the second taxi driver had not been able to figure out where the restaurant was, so he had dropped them off at the Piazza Bologna. Massimo grabbed his car keys immediately and volunteered to pick them up. What a way to start the meal—with true hospitality.

When everyone had arrived, we asked Massimo to make us their specialties. We started with plates of seafood antipasto, which just kept coming. The dishes included mussels with breadcrumbs, crispy anchovies, tender marinated octopus, insalata di mare and shrimp in butter sauce. One dish I had never tasted before was farro, or spelt, which they served like a risotto with seafood. The flavor was unique. They also served us fresh sardines in oil, which were incredibly mild and tasty.

Back at Fork, we enjoy fresh sardines when they are available. *Escabeche* means pickled in vinegar or lime juice. But this dish reminds me a bit more of the marinated anchovies we had in Rome, because it is not so vinegary.

Escabeche generally refers to pickled fish, chicken or vegetables, depending on the origin of the recipe. In Spanish cuisine, the term usually refers to pickled seafood. Pickled peppers and other vegetables are common in Mexican cuisine. Ingredients used in the pickling process generally include olive oil, vinegar, sugar and other seasonings.

sardines escabeche

Serves 6 to 8 as a first course

20 fresh sardines, cleaned, scaled and deheaded if desired

2 sprigs fresh thyme

2 sprigs fresh rosemary

extra-virgin olive oil

2 T white-wine vinegar

Preheat oven to 350°F. Arrange filets in a single layer in a shallow casserole or baking dish. Cover with olive oil until all sardines are submerged; add vinegar and herbs. Place in oven and bake 10 minutes, until oil is just warm. Remove and allow to cool. If dish is not served immediately, refrigerate.

As I said earlier, Massimo and his family did not speak a lot of English, and although a few of us had studied Italian, there were some gaps in our ability to communicate. Yet our shared enthusiasm for food inspired both the Americans and the Italians to make a greater effort to connect that evening. Massimo's family insisted that we have real pasta carbonara. They came over to explain that this dish was authentic because it was made with only eggs and cheese--no cream. Since normally I don't eat anything so rich, even without cream I found this dish way over the top. They followed it with a grilled sea bass, which was very fresh and simple.

At Fork we serve a Mediterranean sea bass called bronzino that is equally mild, flaky and delicious. At the restaurant we serve 1¼ to 1½ pounds of whole fish per person. At home, a two- to three-pound bronzino is likely to serve two to three people. It is easier to serve the whole fish family style.

pan-roasted bronzino

Serves 2 to 4

2- to 3-pound whole bronzino, cleaned, scaled and gutted

2 T olive oil

1 lemon, cut into wedges

salt and black pepper

extra-virgin olive oil and aged balsamic vinegar for drizzling

Preheat oven to 350°F. Heat olive oil in pan. When oil is hot, place fish carefully in pan. Season with salt and pepper. When fish can be easily loosened from pan, turn fish and season second side with salt and pepper. Place pan with fish in oven for 10 minutes. Drizzle with olive oil and balsamic vinegar. Serve with lemon wedges.

At La Cassetta, the fish was served aside braised saffron potatoes and sautéed greens. At Fork, Thien had created a similar braised potato that we use as an accompaniment to any simple meat or chicken dish.

braised potatoes with saffron

Serves 4 as a side dish

2 pounds Yukon gold potatoes

3 cups water

10 saffron threads

¼ cup extra-virgin olive oil

2 cloves garlic, minced

1 small red onion, chopped

½ cup chopped, fresh flat-leaf
    parsley

2 tsp dried oregano

2 T grated pecorino or parmesan

salt and freshly ground black pepper

Preheat oven to 350°F. Place potatoes in water in a large pot. Bring to a boil. Add saffron threads. Remove from heat. Cover and allow to cool. Remove potatoes. Reserve 1 cup of water. With skin on, slice potatoes into ¼-inch slices. Set aside.

In a sauté pan, sauté olive oil, garlic and onions until they are translucent. Add parsley and oregano. Season with salt and pepper. Set aside.

In an 8-by-8-inch baking dish, layer potato slices and cover with sautéed onions and herbs. Add 1 cup of reserved saffron water. Sprinkle with cheese. Cover with aluminum foil. Bake for 45 minutes or until potatoes are tender. Serve warm.

When the staff at La Cassetta mentioned dessert, we all told them that we were stuffed. But I also told them how much I loved Luca's tiramisu at Melograno. They responded by bringing three plates of tiramisu for everyone to share, and of course it was delicious.

6

ASIAN ACCENTS

Thien considers eating out the equivalent of his culinary education.
Of course, another part of dining out for him is checking out the
competition, but it also gives him the opportunity to see what trends,
ideas and combinations are being tried. As Thien's training was hands
on—he didn't go to cooking school—he feels that dining at restaurants
is a relatively inexpensive investment compared to the amount he might
have spent on cooking school. So when he goes out, money is no object.
At times, he has walked into a new restaurant by himself and ordered
everything on the menu. Years ago we went to Trust, the first upscale
tapas restaurant in Philadelphia. There were at least fifty different types
of tapas on the menu. The chef was Guillermo Pernot, with whom
Thien had worked at ¡Pasion! We were a party of three that evening
and the hour was late. Thien said to the waiter, "We'll have one of
everything." Of course the kitchen staff began looking into the dining
room to try to see who had placed this crazy order. But he got what
he asked for; the three of us sat at a table big enough for eight people
with fifty-some plates in front of us, and by the end we had received
an education in tapas.

The types and styles of food Thien tries out run the gamut, from a two-dollar taco to dinner at the most expensive restaurants in town. As his frequent dining companion, I have noticed that his interests are always shifting. When he was on an oyster kick, we went to an oyster bar a few weeks in a row; soon after, we'd have Fork fruits de mer on the menu. If sushi was his passion of the moment, we might eat it several times in a week (or better yet, oysters followed by sushi). Then Thien would make his own interpretations of sushi. For a long period, Vietnamese food was his main concern when we ate out. We would pick the restaurant based on its specialty. If we wanted *pho* (beef noodle soup), then Pho 75, the dive soup bar in South Philadelphia, was the best choice. If we wanted summer rolls, we'd opt for Nam Phuong, also in South Philly, where the rolls are made to order; and for certain types of fresh seafood, such as lobster or Dungeness crab, Pho Xe Lua (pronounced *fo se' lo*) in Chinatown was best.

I was fine with eating at Japanese, Vietnamese, even Malaysian restaurants with Thien, but Chinese was another story. Not that I'm a snob, but I've been spoiled by my mother (a great cook) and my family, which seeks great Chinese food throughout the world. We have eaten in great Chinese restaurants throughout Asia, San Francisco and New York, enjoying the cuisines of many regions. In Philadelphia, as in many Chinatowns in the United States, the majority of Chinese restaurants are Cantonese. There are many great Cantonese restaurants, but many have similar menus, and the banquet menu, if there is one, is usually written in Chinese. Due to my own inability to read Chinese, I usually can't order from it, as the waiters do not have the time or patience to translate and explain. In addition, I don't like eating Chinese food unless I can share it with my dining companions. Chinese food is meant to be eaten family style. If you can't agree on dishes that everyone will like, it's no fun. But I am accustomed to eating jellyfish, oxtail, whole duck and so on, and I find it boring to eat the stereotypic Chinese-American dishes. However, I will eat with Thien at his favorite Chinese restaurant, Tai Lake, because

I love fresh seafood, which is their specialty. And Thien has introduced me to a few things that my family doesn't order, such as snails with black bean sauce. His other favorite is beef chow fun. But even when Thien eats Chinese food, he orders the same things every time!

Thien used to say to me, "You're so American." I would get so annoyed because, like every person born of first-generation immigrants, I have struggled with my identity. One of Fork's ironies is that the restaurant is an American bistro and both Thien and I are Asian Americans. Because we are Asian American, many potential guests have asked me over the years whether the restaurant is a Chinese restaurant, or how long Thien and I have been married, or if we are related in some way. Once a guest protested that she had made a reservation even though we didn't have it in our book. When she saw me across the room, she told the hostess that she had spoken to a woman with an Asian accent. My staff laughed. Since I was born in the United States, the only accent I have is from northern New Jersey.

When Thien first arrived and proposed menu items with Asian ingredients, I was concerned that people might interpret the menu as being solely Asian. As a result, when he introduced these dishes, I counterbalanced them with an equal number of Mediterranean and Latino flavors. At first, Thien would introduce just a twist of an Asian influence when he made classic European recipes. For example, Thai basil is an herb from Vietnamese cuisine that Thien incorporated into his cooking at Fork. It is more pungent and peppery than Italian basil, and it ties in perfectly with our seasonal concept, since Judy and Mark Dornstreich of Branch Creek Farm grow it.

The coulis in the recipe that follows could be served with numerous other dishes, including scallops and other types of seafood. The lamb goes well with roasted potatoes and sautéed haricots verts.

roasted rack of lamb with red-wine reduction, thai-basil coulis and hazelnuts

Serves 4 as a dinner main course

THAI-BASIL COULIS

3 bunches fresh Thai basil, stems removed (about 1½ cups leaves)

4 bunches fresh parsley, stems included

¼ cup lemon juice

¼ cup honey

¼ cup canola oil

½ cup extra-virgin olive oil

Combine Thai basil, parsley, lemon juice and honey in a food processor and process until ingredients are chopped fine. With processor running, add oils in a slow, steady stream. Add 1 teaspoon salt, mix well to combine and set aside.

LAMB

10 whole garlic cloves

5 shallots, chopped

1 bunch fresh thyme

1 bunch fresh rosemary

1½ cups canola oil (more as needed to cover meat)

3-pound rack of lamb (about 2½ baby racks)

Mix ingredients together and pour over lamb in a glass baking dish or bowl. Cover and let marinate at least 1 hour.

Kosher salt

freshly ground black pepper

½ cup hazelnuts, toasted and coarsely ground

Preheat oven to 400°F. Remove lamb from marinade and season with salt and pepper. Discard marinade. Heat a large pan (not nonstick) over medium-high heat. Add lamb and sear on each side, about 3 minutes per side. Transfer pan with lamb to oven and finish to desired temperature (15 to 20 minutes for medium rare). Set hazelnuts aside.

RED-WINE REDUCTION

1½ cups red wine

¾ cup demi-glace (veal or beef; see recipe in Fork Foundations or use store-bought)

1 tsp honey

1 T butter

Remove lamb from roasting pan and tent with foil to keep warm. Deglaze pan with wine and simmer over high heat until reduced by half. Add demi-glace, stir to combine well and simmer an additional 5 minutes or until liquid has been reduced into a thick sauce. Turn off heat and swirl in 1 tablespoon of butter to finish sauce.

To assemble, remove meat from pan and let stand about 10 minutes before slicing it into individual chops. To serve, sauce plate with red-wine reduction, along with other sides or vegetables if desired. Arrange five chops per plate leaning against vegetables. Sprinkle with toasted hazelnuts and drizzle with Thai-basil coulis.

Thai basil is a variety of basil often used in Southeast Asian cooking. Unlike its Italian counterpart, Thai basil has deep-green leaves with purplish flower buds and a licorice-anise flavor. It is readily available in Asian markets and can be grown easily in an herb garden, even in the northeastern United States.

Grilled grape leaves stuffed with beef are one of my favorite Vietnamese specialties. I love the charred flavor of the leaves. They are dipped in fish sauce that contains a little rice-wine vinegar. From time to time, Thien makes this traditional starter with beef or lamb. This particular recipe is a variation. The grape leaves, coupled with the mint in the rice, remind me of Vietnamese cuisine, yet the dish could also be interpreted as Mediterranean.

grilled quail wrapped in grape leaves with stuffing of pine nuts, mint and rice

Serves 4 as a dinner appetizer or a light lunch

GRILLED QUAIL

1½ cups extra-virgin olive oil

3 cloves garlic, peeled, smashed

1 T fresh rosemary, chopped

1 T fresh thyme, chopped

2 T shallots, chopped fine

4 quail, chest bones removed

6 to 8 grape leaves, rinsed and dried

Mix all marinade ingredients together and marinate quail for 2 hours. Set grape leaves aside.

STUFFING

1 cup jasmine rice, cooked al dente

3 T pine nuts, toasted

¼ cup fresh mint leaves, chopped fine

salt and black pepper

Mix rice, pine nuts, mint, salt and pepper together in a bowl. Set aside. Heat and oil grill. Preheat oven to 375°F. Remove quails from marinade and stuff chest cages with rice stuffing. Wrap each quail with 1 or 2 grape leaves. Skewer quail if necessary to hold quail and grape leaves together. Place quail on hot grill. After quails are well marked, transfer to oven in a roasting pan and roast for 5 minutes for medium.

SALAD

frisée, cleaned

½ cup olive oil

2 T lemon juice

salt and freshly ground black pepper to taste

In a small bowl, whisk olive oil, lemon juice, salt and pepper. Dress frisée.

To assemble, place each quail on a small bed of frisée.

Over time, Thien started introducing menu items that clearly had an Asian palate. When he started the special Sunday-night dinners, things started changing in the cooking he did for us on those nights. Maybe he thought that if I tasted the Asian dishes, I would be more likely to accept them on the menu. He included Asian greens and herbs, dried mushrooms and more exotic ingredients. This recipe was one of the first dishes he made at Sunday-night dinner that made it onto the restaurant menu. It is easy and delicious, and the anchovy flavor is not strong. When we put it onto the restaurant menu, it became popular immediately.

Malanga is a root vegetable very similar to taro root. Usually it has a tough, brown, shaggy skin and is the size of a white potato. Prior to deep frying, soak it in water to remove excess starch. The malanga's skin can be peeled with a vegetable peeler.

steamed clams with sherry, chinese watercress and anchovy

Serves 4 as a dinner appetizer or 2 as a lunch entrée

2 T olive oil

4 cloves garlic, minced

40 little neck clams, washed

1 cup sherry

2 bunches watercress, washed

1 T anchovy paste

Heat a tall pot. Add olive oil. Sauté garlic and anchovy in pot until garlic is caramelized. Add clams and cover pot to steam clams. When clams have opened, deglaze pan with sherry. Add watercress. (Watercress does not need to be completely wilted.) Stir and serve in bowl.

Thien prepared this dish at a Sunday-night dinner after one of our sushi dinners out on the town. Since the popularization of sushi, tuna tartare has become a popular dish on many restaurant menus. It is so commonplace that we had to look for a way to make it more unusual.

This marinade is a little more unusual than the soy-sesame marinade often served. It uses coconut milk as well as fish sauce, an important ingredient in Vietnamese cooking. I don't use fish sauce in my own cooking because I don't care for the smell. But if fish sauce is used correctly, the finished product generally doesn't have a strong aroma. And if I don't have to smell it, I'm happy to eat dishes that contain it! Fish sauce is made from fermented anchovies. As is true with white truffle oil, if you use too much, its intense flavors can easily overpower a dish.

In any case, this tuna tartare dish is one of my favorites. As a passed hors d'oeuvre, it is always a crowd pleaser. It is imperative that you use fresh, sushi-grade tuna. If you can't find culandro (a milder version of cilantro), use a teaspoon of chopped cilantro.

The notion of serving foods **tartare** is believed to have originated in Russia. According to legend, warriors would put meat under their horses' saddles, ride as usual and eat the meat once it had been tenderized by their horses' motion. Nowadays, "tartare" usually refers to a raw meat or fish that is coarsely ground or chopped fine.

coconut-lime tuna tartare with crispy malanga chips

Makes approximately 16 pieces as an hors d'oeuvre or serves 4 as an appetizer

COCONUT-LIME TUNA TARTARE

½ can coconut milk

1 T fish sauce

½ jalapeño pepper, seeded and minced

1 T culandro, chiffonade

¼ cup lime juice

½ pound ahi tuna loin, cut into ¼-inch dice

In a bowl, whisk coconut milk, fish sauce, pepper, culandro and lime juice. Add tuna cubes and gently mix.

CRISPY MALANGA CHIPS

1 malanga root, peeled, then shaved with a Japanese mandoline into rounds

2 cups canola oil

salt and freshly ground black pepper

chives or baby greens

Heat oil in a Dutch oven or large pot until it registers 365°F on a deep-fry thermometer. Working in batches to avoid overcrowding, carefully drop malanga rounds into hot oil and fry until golden. Scoop chips out with a slotted spoon or tongs. Transfer

to a cooling rack lined with paper towels to drain excess oil. Season with salt and pepper.

If serving as an hors d'oeuvre, place ½ teaspoon to 1 teaspoon of tuna tartare on top of each malanga chip. Place on serving plate. Garnish with chives or baby greens. If serving as an appetizer at table, divide tartare onto four plates. Garnish with malanga chips and chives or baby greens.

Another simple Asian recipe that Thien introduced to us one Sunday night was this tasty sautéed salmon dish. Be careful not to put too much sauce on the fish. The Caramelized Soy-Ginger Sauce is very salty after being reduced, so a little goes a long way.

How to Cook Rice

Cooking rice properly is one of the most difficult tasks in Asian cooking. Rice that is too hard or undercooked is undesirable, but rice that is too mushy is not acceptable, either. When rice is cooked properly, the single kernels should be identifiable. A rice cooker can help ensure that steamed rice is made perfectly, but if you don't have a rice cooker, you can make perfect rice on your stovetop. These instructions apply to white rice only. First, rinse rice by putting it into a big pot with cold water. Carefully pour off water and repeat until water is clear. Place rice and water in a rice cooker and follow manufacturer's instructions, or cook on stovetop as follows: Bring water to a boil. If you wish to salt your water, do so at this time. Add rice. Stir so that rice does not stick to bottom. After 2 minutes, reduce heat to low and cover. Cook for 10 to 15 minutes. Remove from heat and keep covered an additional 15 minutes, or until liquid is absorbed and rice is done.

sautéed salmon with caramelized soy-ginger sauce, roasted bell peppers and steamed sushi rice with peanuts aside baby bok choy

Serves 4 people as a dinner main course

STEAMED SUSHI RICE WITH PEANUTS

1 cup sushi rice

2¼ cup water

½ cup coconut milk

1 scallion, chopped fine

¼ cup chopped peanuts

Steam rice in a rice cooker or on stovetop (see sidebar). Before serving, mix in coconut milk and scallions. Set peanuts aside.

ROASTED BELL PEPPERS

1 red bell pepper, cored and seeded

1 yellow bell pepper, cored and seeded

2 T canola oil

Preheat oven to 450°F. Cut peppers into squares, 1 inch by 1 inch. Toss peppers with canola oil and spread them onto a sheet pan covered with foil. Roast for 8 minutes.

CARAMELIZED SOY-GINGER SAUCE

¾ cup soy sauce

½ cup sugar

½ cup fish stock

3 cloves garlic

3-inch piece of ginger, peeled and cut into ¼-inch-thick coins

1 jalapeño, seeded

1 shallot, minced

Place all ingredients in a medium pot and simmer for 15 minutes. Remove from heat and blend ingredients in a blender or food processor or in a pot using a burr mixer. Strain mixture through a fine-mesh strainer, catching liquid in a clean saucepan. Return sauce to stovetop and boil to reduce further, about 10 to 15 minutes. Sauce should have viscosity of maple syrup. Keep warm until ready to use.

BABY BOK CHOY

4 baby bok choy, washed and halved

salt and freshly ground black pepper to taste

Fill a large saucepan with water and bring to a boil. Season water generously with salt. Add bok choy and blanch, uncovered, for about 5 minutes. Remove from water, drain, season with salt and pepper and keep warm until ready to serve.

SAUTÉED SALMON

4 filets of salmon, approximately 6 ounces each

2 tsp olive oil

Heat olive oil in a large sauté pan over high heat. Do not season salmon, as sauce is already salty. Sear salmon (skin side up if there is skin) in pan on one side for 2 minutes over high heat. Reduce heat to medium and cook an additional 3 minutes. Turn fish over and continue cooking over medium heat to desired temperature, approximately 3 minutes for medium rare. Keep warm.

To assemble the dish, heat soy-ginger sauce in pan. Add pepper chunks and toss to coat and warm them through. Place rice and bok choy on plate. Sprinkle rice with chopped peanuts. Place salmon over rice and spoon peppers over salmon. Drizzle an additional teaspoon of sauce on top. Garnish with chervil or other microgreen.

As I said, Thien's Sunday-night dinner is not just a family meal; it is a way for us to taste new menu items and wines. Over time I realized that Thien was not only introducing us to a new palate; he was also using Sunday nights as a way to educate us about his culture--either that or just to indulge his desire to shock! One memorable dinner included an aspiring restaurateur and a managing editor from *Philadelphia Magazine* along with the usual five suspects--me, Wayne, Roberto, Roberto's date and Thien. This particular dinner began with duck eggs, which seemed harmless when he had first described them. Thien had explained that the eggs provided all the protein a person needed in a day, and that he and his mom used to eat three each morning. But when they arrived in a bowl with no pretense whatsoever, we saw that the eggs were double the size of chicken eggs and hard boiled. And to eat them, we had to crack a small hole at the top, remove the embryonic lining, sip the broth from the shell, sprinkle the inside with salt and pepper and spoon the embryo right out of the egg! That's right, the embryo. Thien explained that the embryos were 18 days gestated. At that point, everyone stopped trying to open their eggs for a moment. Then we continued, however, spurred by the wish to be good dinner guests. The broth was the richest duck consommé I've had. The embryo looked like a baby duck, but if you closed your eyes while you ate it, it tasted like a wonderfully rich and tender piece of duck breast.

The following week, with just the five of us, Thien announced that he had made another Vietnamese specialty. He brought out a big bowl of pickled duck tongue. Roberto had had enough! Although he loved Sunday-night dinner as a concept, these dinners were becoming much too adventurous, even for Roberto. He begged me to discourage Thien from making these very unusual dishes. So I asked Thien to focus on those items that might actually make it to the Fork menu.

the necklace and noodle rolls

In 2003, to celebrate my thirty-eighth birthday, my mom, my brother Ken, Wayne, Thien and I had lunch at Pho Xe Lua, Thien's favorite Vietnamese restaurant in Chinatown, which serves amazing seafood. At that time I hadn't been there yet, so I was a little concerned because my family members are tough customers. But Thien insisted. My mom had never eaten Vietnamese food before but was willing to try it. The event was a huge success. After this lunch, my family stopped eating Chinese food in Chinatown and now eats only at Vietnamese restaurants in Philadelphia. My mom loves the freshness and flavors of this cuisine, especially the Thai basil and mint.

During that particular lunch, Thien threw a small box at me that looked like it contained jewelry and mumbled "Happy Birthday." I opened the box and saw that it contained a gold necklace with a pendant containing jade and a small diamond. It was simple and very elegant.

Thien explained that when he was about sixteen, he went to Paris to study and lived with a French artist and his Vietnamese wife. He stayed in their home, and he cleaned the atelier to earn his keep. Secretly he was in love with Monique, the Vietnamese wife. As he was preparing to return to Vietnam to his mother, he thought to himself, "How can I impress Monique?" He decided that if he bought his mother a gift and solicited Monique's help in selecting it, she would be touched that he would want to buy a beautiful memento for his mom. Monique knew exactly where to buy this extremely special gift: an old French antique store. The two chose the very necklace I was holding, which Thien had brought back to Vietnam for his mother.

But when he presented it to his mom, she was not impressed. She told Thien that he should have saved the money and sent it home instead. Through all the years of war and turmoil, she never wore it, but she

Women rule (left to right: Ashley Cobbett Stafford, Amanda Pfeifer, Ellen, Samantha Fratangelo, Lauren Derstine)

did keep it safe. It has a gold chain with a soft clasp. When you hook it together, you just squeeze the gold clasp to close the necklace.

I was extremely flattered and touched that Thien would give me something with such sentimental value. Generally I don't accessorize, and only rarely do I wear jewelry; most days, a watch or a necklace is it! If I do wear a necklace, I often leave it on for days. After lunch that day, I put on the necklace and left it on for a few weeks.

It was summertime then, and Thien had a culinary idea new to Fork: to use fresh rice noodles. He used the flat, ribbon-like noodles used to make chow fun, a noodle stir-fry often made with beef or chicken. A market in Chinatown makes them on the premises exceptionally well. The shelf life of the noodles is short; as they age, they get more inflexible. Thien was wrapping the fresh noodles around cucumber and herbs and called the resulting item a rice pillow. So for his new dish to be really good, we had to pick fresh noodles up from the store every day. I never minded doing this task, because I'd usually stop to eat a box of steamed noodles with sesame paste and soy sauce while I was there.

One day I rode my bike to pick up the noodles. Between Market Street and Chinatown I took all kinds of short cuts to avoid riding my bike down Market Street, a busy thoroughfare, as much as possible. I was wearing the necklace that Thien had given me. On the way home, I felt the chain fall into my blouse. I stopped short and realized that the worst had happened: the pendant had fallen off the necklace. I backtracked to the noodle shop in search of the pendant, with no success. I felt horrible. How could I have lost something of such enormous sentimental value?

I returned to the restaurant with my head down, utterly depressed. Thien tried not to act upset, but I knew he was. He tried to be encouraging, saying, "It'll turn up, and if it doesn't it's probably somewhere around here, and my mom's spirit will always be here." Despite his words, I couldn't sleep that night.

The next morning I got up early to give it one more try when there was less traffic. I walked from Fork up Market Street, looking into every nook and cranny in the road. Just when I was about to give up hope, I thought I saw something green at the corner of Seventh and Market. I leaned down, and there was the small pendant in perfect condition, stuck in between two clay bricks in the middle of the bus lane on Market Street. I literally ran back to the restaurant, screaming for Thien. We were all ecstatic, but I haven't worn the necklace since.

This recipe for grilled hamachi and rice-noodle rolls was the dish that almost took away the necklace. There are many variations on this rice-noodle roll, including putting salmon sashimi or smoked duck inside the roll or substituting cucumber or green mango for the papaya. If you can't get the noodles fresh, you can steam them right before serving and eat them immediately.

grilled hamachi with rice-noodle rolls, green papaya and scallion-lime coulis

Serves 6 as an appetizer

Hamachi, also known as Japanese amberjack or yellowtail tuna, is often used to make sushi. The fish can be found in the wild or farmed.

SCALLION-LIME COULIS

1 T minced ginger

3 bunches scallions, chopped

⅓ cup lemon juice

1 T fish sauce

1 cup extra-virgin olive oil

1 T fresh basil, chopped

salt and freshly ground black pepper
   to taste

Place ginger, scallions, lemon juice and fish sauce in a food processor and pulse several times. With processor running, add oil in a slow, steady stream. Add chopped basil and salt and pepper to taste. Set aside.

GRILLED HAMACHI WITH RICE-NOODLE ROLLS

1 pound hamachi filets

½ cup olive oil

salt and freshly ground black pepper

½ pound fresh rice-noodle sheets
   (available at Asian markets)

1 cup julienned green papaya

¼ cup fresh mint leaves

¼ cup fresh basil leaves

¼ cup fresh cilantro leaves

1 head bibb lettuce, torn into pieces

Preheat grill. While grill preheats, marinate hamachi filets in olive oil. When grill is hot, season fish with salt and pepper and place it on grill. Wait until fish pulls away from grill easily to turn it, after approximately 4 to 5 minutes. Grill an additional 4 minutes on other side for medium rare.

To make a roll, place a noodle on a plate and on the bottom third of the noodle (the part closest to you) arrange small pieces of fish; some green papaya; a few mint, basil and cilantro leaves and some lettuce. Be careful not to overstuff noodle roll. Roll noodle away from you into a tight, 1-inch-thick roll. Cut into 1-inch, bite-sized pieces. Spoon 1 tablespoon of Scallion-Lime Coulis onto each plate. Evenly divide rolls between plates, placing them so that when you look down on the plate, you are looking at the insides of the rolls. Garnish with baby greens or Thai basil leaves.

korean kick

In his everexpanding quest for novel food experiences, Thien decided he
needed to try Korean barbecue. So he suggested we go to the section of
Philadelphia known as Korea Town and look around. We had heard that
a restaurant called Kim's served great barbecue.

The main drag of Korea Town is North Fifth Street in the Olney section
of North Philadelphia. The drive up from Old City is not Philadelphia's
most scenic. Olney is a working-class neighborhood that has deteriorated
over the past fifty years. Not knowing exactly where Kim's was, we looked
for a concentration of signs in Korean, then parked. We saw a few small
Korean restaurants, but none of them served Korean barbecue and
their staffs didn't speak English. Finally, we stopped in a Vietnamese
restaurant, where the staff told us that Kim's was a few blocks up the
street. Still, we had no address or clear idea of where we were going.
As we walked farther and farther, the neighborhood grew more and
more residential. Just when I was ready to give up, we smelled the aroma
of grilled meat. The restaurant was in an old diner. Each table had a
barbecue "pit" in its middle that held a grill with hot wood coals in it.
An exhaust hood was built into the restaurant's ceiling to remove cooking
odors. The waitresses were Chinese Koreans who had emigrated during
the Korean War. They spoke very little English but did speak Korean and
Chinese. Once they learned that I could speak Chinese, they became
friendly to us. We might have seemed a bit unusual, because we had our
own wine glasses and a bottle of wine. Thien had brought a great bottle
of red that matched beautifully with the grilled short ribs, beef tongue
and spicy pork we ordered.

Typically, Korean restaurants serve a variety of little cold dishes such as kimchi at the beginning of a meal. After experiencing Korean barbecue, Thien adopted this tradition for several of our Wednesday-night dinners. He created other dishes as a result of our barbecue dinners as well. The basis of all of them was his adaptation of Korean barbecue sauce.

spicy korean pork chops with kimchi and sushi rice

Serves 4 as a dinner main course

QUICK KIMCHI

2 cups white vinegar

5 cloves garlic, smashed to a paste with 1 tsp coarse salt

2 T sugar

2 tsp red-pepper flakes

1 tsp hondashi (bonito fish stock, available bottled)

1 head (2 to 3 pounds) Napa or Savoy cabbage, sliced crosswise into ½-inch strips

2 cucumbers, seeded and julienned

1 bunch scallions, sliced thin

Combine cabbage, cucumber and scallions in a 13-by-9-inch glass baking dish. Mix vinegar, garlic, sugar, red-pepper flakes and hondashi in a medium saucepan and bring to a boil. When it is boiling, pour liquid over cabbage mixture. Cover baking dish with plastic wrap and weigh down with a heavy pan or smaller baking dish. Refrigerate 3 to 4 hours.

KOREAN BARBECUE SAUCE

3 Asian pears, peeled and cored

¼ cup walnuts

1 tsp sesame oil

⅔ cup soy sauce

¼ cup corn syrup

3 T sugar

1 to 2 jalapeño peppers (depending on desired spiciness), tops removed

4 cloves garlic

¼ cup fresh cilantro leaves

1 small Spanish onion, cut into large chunks

4 scallions

3-inch-piece of ginger root, peeled and chopped

Place all ingredients in a food processor or blender. Cover with canola oil. Purée. Refrigerate until ready to use.

SUSHI RICE

2 cups sushi rice

2 cups water

salt and freshly ground black pepper to taste

Follow manufacturer's instructions for rice steamer or cook rice on stovetop (see sidebar on page 208).

PORK CHOPS

4 bone-in center pork chops, French cut

1 quart fresh orange juice

salt and freshly ground black pepper

Marinate pork in orange juice for a minimum of 6 hours. When ready to cook them, preheat grill. Season pork chops with salt and pepper. Place on hot grill. Baste with about 1 cup barbecue sauce. Cook 6 to 7 minutes on each side for medium rare. Remove chops from grill and brush with additional barbecue sauce before serving with steamed sushi rice and kimchi.

7

LATINO INFLUENCES

You may remember that when Thien first arrived, I asked him to assist then-chef Dave Ballentine with menu ideas. Because I didn't know Thien well, understanding his vision of a new dish was sometimes challenging. When he wrote an idea on paper, I would have a certain vision in my head, but when he made the dish, it would be completely different. And many of his ideas were too much of a departure from our existing menu. Some required ingredients that we did not keep in house or involved combinations that I viewed at the time as too much like fusion cuisine. His suggested dishes often mixed aspects of Latin, French and Asian cuisines. This influence was only natural, since Thien had worked with Guillermo Pernot at the nuevo-Latino restaurant ¡Pasion! prior to working at Fork.

The recipe that follows is one of his most successful in that category. Roberto kept saying to me that there was one ingredient too many in every dish. But over time, I realized that this was chiefly a matter of wording. Thien's recipes often began with a classic recipe and gave it a minor modification. So if I gave a dish a simpler name that was more familiar, it worked on the menu. This dish, for instance, is a variation on steak frites.

smoked rib-eye steak with guava red-wine reduction, pickled ramps and taro frites

Serves 4 as a dinner main course

GUAVA RED-WINE REDUCTION

3 cups meat stock (see recipe in Fork Foundations or use store-bought)

1 cup burgundy wine

1 dried Mexican red pepper, rehydrated

3 T guava concentrate or honey

2 T cognac

Reduce all ingredients together to one-third. Strain. Return to stovetop, add cognac and reduce by half. Set aside.

PICKLED RAMPS

2 bunches ramps

1 cup white vinegar

2 T sugar

2 tsp salt

1 bay leaf

1/4 tsp freshly ground black pepper

Boil a pot of water. Blanch ramps in water for 1½ minutes. Mix white vinegar, sugar, salt, bay leaves and pepper together in an airtight container. Add blanched ramps and close. Ramps can be kept in pickling fluid in refrigerator for up to a month.

SMOKED RIB-EYE STEAK

3 T ancho chili powder

1½ T paprika

3 T poblano chili powder

1 T ground coriander

1 T ground cumin

2 tsp garlic powder

2 tsp onion powder

2 to 3 T olive oil

four 12-ounce rib-eye or Delmonico steaks

Combine spices together with olive oil into a paste. Rub each rib-eye with paste on both sides. Smoke steak for 8 minutes. Remove from smoker. Season steak well with salt and pepper. Grill 7 minutes on one side. Turn and grill an additional 6 minutes for medium rare.

TARO FRITES

1 pound taro

water

3 cups canola oil

¼ cup all-purpose flour

1 T paprika

Kosher salt

freshly ground black pepper

Put taro (with skin on) in a large pot and cover it with water. Bring water to a boil, then turn off heat. Let taro sit in water until it is cool enough to touch. Remove taro and peel skin using a paring knife. Cut taro into halves or quarters, depending on size.

Put oil in a deep pot and heat to 365°F. Mix flour and paprika together. Dip taro pieces into flour mixture. When oil is hot, drop taro in and fry until golden, about 2 to 3 minutes. Carefully remove from oil with a spider basket or slotted spoon, toss in salt and pepper and serve aside steak.

Ramps are wild leeks that are in season in the early spring. Ramps have a thin, white bulb resembling that of a scallion and a flat green leaf like the leaves of a leek.

Variations on the Smoking Process

The smoking process adds another dimension to this rib-eye dish. If you are short on time, a rub of the herbs listed will suffice. And if you don't have a smoker, you can still smoke the rib eye outside in a barbecue grill that has a cover. First place the steaks on the cold grill. Then take an old pan and place a handful of hickory chips in it. Light the chips on fire. Place the pan on the grill with the steaks and close the top of the barbecue grill. Wait 10 minutes, then open the grill. You have smoked rib eye!

red-wine-braised pork shank, moros christian rice with black beans and sautéed watercress

Serves 4 as a dinner main course

PORK SHANK

1 T salt

1 T sugar

½ cup water

1 cup orange juice

¼ tsp vanilla extract

4 pork shanks

2 T olive oil

1 carrot, coarsely chopped

1 stalk celery, coarsely chopped

1 white onion, coarsely chopped

2 cloves garlic, whole

2 T tomato paste

1 cup burgundy wine

2 cups orange juice

3 cups meat or chicken stock (see recipe in Fork Foundations or use store-bought)

2 star anise, whole

6 whole cloves

5 parsley stems

1 bunch fresh thyme

1 bunch fresh rosemary

cheesecloth and butcher's string

1 dried ancho chili

1 cup orange juice

1 cup fresh parsley leaves

Dissolve salt and sugar in water in a small saucepan over low heat. Transfer to a large bowl or container and add orange juice, vanilla extract and shanks. Add cold water to cover and marinate shanks in brine for a minimum of 2 days.

Preheat oven to 350°F. Heat oil in a large skillet over medium-high heat. Sauté carrot, celery, onion until caramelized. Stir in garlic and tomato paste and cook an additional minute. Transfer mixture to a roasting pan. Remove shanks from braising liquid and add to roasting pan. Cover shanks with wine, orange juice and stock. Place star anise, clove, parsley, thyme and rosemary in a cheesecloth, tie together and add to liquid. Add ancho chili and parsley. Cover with aluminum foil. Braise in oven for 3 hours.

After braising, remove from heat and let shanks cool in braising liquid. Remove shanks from braising liquid and skim fat off which should float to top of liquid. Strain liquid through chinois or mesh strainer. Reduce liquid in a small saucepan over medium heat until thickened, about 20 minutes.

MOROS CHRISTIAN RICE WITH BLACK BEANS

¾ cup black beans, cooked to firm (see sidebar on page 37; save water from cooking beans)

1 T olive oil

¼ cup uncooked bacon, diced

¼ cup white onions, diced

¼ cup red bell pepper, diced

2 cloves garlic, minced

1 cup jasmine rice, unwashed

1 tsp ground cumin

salt and freshly ground black pepper to taste

Preheat oven to 350°F. Heat olive oil in a medium sauté pan over medium high heat. Add bacon and cook until crisp. Add onions and pepper and sauté until just soft and fragrant. Stir in garlic, cooking 1 minute more. Stir in rice, cumin, salt, pepper and beans. Add enough water to reserved bean cooking liquid to equal 2 cups. Pour into rice and bean mixture and bring to boil. Cover with foil and transfer to oven for 25 minutes.

SAUTÉED WATERCRESS

1 bunch watercress, cleaned

1 T olive oil

salt and freshly ground black pepper to taste

Heat olive oil in a large sauté pan. Add watercress and toss in olive oil. Season with salt and pepper. Remove from heat and allow watercress to wilt.

To serve, place rice in a large pasta bowl. Place shank in bowl. Drizzle reduced sauce over shank. Add wilted watercress.

Braised pork shank is a dish that almost every culture has a take on, including Asian, French, Italian and Latino. Moros y Cristianos is the traditional name of a Cuban, Puerto Rican and Dominican recipe for black beans and rice. The black beans are said to represent the Moors who invaded the Iberian Peninsula (Spain and Portugal), and the white rice is considered to represent the Christians.

family meal

When Thien worked at ¡Pasion! he met several native Mexicans who were extremely talented cooks. Over time, many of them were hired for positions at Fork because they had liked working with Thien. While usually Thien made a family meal for his kitchen staff eventually he got too busy and began assigning the responsibility to staff members. In addition to being a task that everyone enjoys, the job of cooking the staff meal gives our cooks an opportunity to show Thien and me how their skills are coming along. Eduarda was one of the Mexican cooks we hired, and whenever she cooked, I'd be curious.

Before these cooks had started working at Fork, we'd had some basic Tex-Mex-style items on our menu, such as quesadillas and stuffed peppers. But once they began to show us the range of what was possible, we expanded our offerings and changed how we did the basics. The sauces, salsas, soups and variations of Mexican cuisine that our cooks served at the family meal were introduced gradually to the menu. Even staples such as guacamole and pico de gallo (salsa) can be made with a difference!

This guacamole is great to serve at a party or aside tacos, salads or quesadillas. As an opener to our Sunday-night dinner, we would often enjoy a bowl of guacamole and tortilla chips. We could tell when our favorite guacamole maker, Marisol, wasn't in the kitchen. From time

to time, Roberto would make a special trip to the restaurant to ask if
Marisol could make guacamole for a dinner Roberto was making at home.
If the guacamole she made was particularly spicy, Roberto would joke
hopefully that Marisol—who is quite beautiful—must have been jealous
of his date. Here is our house guacamole recipe, which is based on the
one Marisol used.

fork guacamole and hand-cut tortilla chips

Makes approximately 1 cup

FORK GUACAMOLE

2 ripe avocados

1 cup fresh cilantro leaves, washed, minced fine

1 jalapeño pepper, seeded and minced

1 T fresh lime juice

2 T red onion, minced

1 clove garlic, minced

¼ tsp cumin

1 tsp Kosher salt

freshly ground black pepper

Spoon avocado out of its shell and into a bowl. Mash avocado with a fork to form a chunky paste. Do not overmash. Fold in remaining ingredients.

HAND-CUT TORTILLA CHIPS

9-inch corn tortillas, cut into quarters or eighths

2 cups canola oil

salt and freshly ground black pepper

Heat oil in a Dutch oven or large pot until it registers 365°F on a deep-fry thermometer. Working in batches to avoid overcrowding, carefully drop tortillas into hot oil and fry until golden. Scoop tortillas out with a slotted spoon, spider or tongs. Transfer to a cooling rack lined with paper towels to drain excess oil. Season with salt and pepper.

We learned a great deal about tapas on that night when Thien ordered every dish on the menu at Trust. After that evening, Thien thought that we should serve tapas. During slow periods at Fork:etc, he would even insist that the store's concept wasn't going to work and suggest that we turn it into a tapas bar. While we didn't make that change, we do have a tapas menu at Fork that offers about ten dishes. This tapas item was inspired by one of my favorite family meals from the kitchen: *albondigas*, which are savory Mexican meatballs cooked in a tomato-based sauce or soup. Do not pack the meatballs too tightly; they should be loose and light, not dense. You can substitute beef or pork for the lamb.

lamb albondigas (mexican meatballs)

Makes twenty-two 2-ounce meatballs

LAMB ALBONDIGAS

2 pounds ground lamb

salt and freshly ground black pepper to taste

4 T fresh cilantro

1 small Spanish onion, minced

4 cloves garlic, minced

3 T uncooked Carolina long-grain rice

1 T ground cumin

1 T ground coriander

2 tsp salt

1 tsp black pepper

Mix together all ingredients except meat. Sprinkle mixture over meat and gently mix to incorporate herbs, spices, onions and rice throughout meat, being careful not to overwork. Form 2-ounce balls, barely packing meat together. The rice will bind the meatballs as they cook.

SAUCE

2 pounds plum tomatoes

6 cloves garlic

¼ cup fresh cilantro

2 jalapeño, seeded, or 4-ounce can chipotle peppers

juice of 1 lime (about 2 T)

½ cup water

2 tsp salt

Fill a large pot with water and bring to a boil. Gently drop in tomatoes and boil until skin starts to split. Drain water, add remaining ingredients and purée sauce in pot or transfer in batches to purée in a blender or food processor. Put puréed sauce back in pot if necessary and adjust seasoning. Bring sauce to a boil and drop in meatballs. Reduce to a simmer, cover and cook 30 minutes or until rice is al dente. Serve with sauce as a soup.

One of our signature dinner entrées is the grilled hanger steak with chimichurri. It has been on our menu every night since Thien joined us. Roberto orders the hanger steak about 75 percent of the time when he has a chance to order off the menu. Chimichurri is an Argentinian sauce or marinade that is usually made from herbs such as parsley and oregano, along with garlic and olive oil. Argentina was colonized by the Spaniards in the 1500's, and many European immigrants have moved there since then, including Italians. So this creates some interesting foodways. It seems to me that chimichurri could be compared to a Genovese pesto.

Thien's recipe for the dish follows. He adds ginger, cilantro and scallions to give his chimichurri an Asian twist. He skewers the steak on sugar cane, which can't be eaten. But if you suck on the sugar cane, you will taste the sweetness.

grilled beef skewers marinated in chimichurri

Makes approximately sixteen 2-ounce pieces

CHIMICHURRI

¼ cup lime juice

1 cup fresh cilantro leaves

1 cup fresh parsley leaves

½ cup scallions, roughly chopped

3-inch piece of ginger, peeled and minced

4 cloves garlic

1 shallot

1 jalapeño, destemmed and seeded

¾ cup olive oil

Put all ingredients except olive oil in bowl of a food processor and process to a coarse paste. Transfer to a bowl and whisk in olive oil.

BEEF SKEWERS

2 pounds hanger, flank or skirt steak, trimmed and cut into 2-inch cubes

fifteen or so 3-inch sugar-cane skewers, carved to a point at bottom

Kosher salt and freshly ground black pepper to taste

Marinate steak cubes in chimichurri for 1 hour (reserving ¼ cup of sauce for topping grilled meat, if desired). Do not marinate too long, because hanger steak will start to become tough. Preheat grill. Skewer beef on sugar canes and season generously with salt and pepper. Transfer skewers to hot grill and cook approximately 3 minutes per side, depending on desired doneness.

wednesday-night dinner

As mentioned, our Wednesday-night chef's bistro dinner at Fork:etc
is one venue for Thien's experimentation. These meals give us all the
perfect opportunity to determine how guests will respond to new menu
items, especially those with a stronger ethnic bent. The dinner includes
four courses and wine. Thien sets the menu each Wednesday morning,
and we post it on the Internet for people to view that day. Since we take
no reservations, we are never certain how many people will show up
or who they will be. When we first started, many people were skeptical
about this chance to try something new. They feared that they wouldn't
get seated or might be allergic to the foods served. Some simply couldn't
accept not being able to control what they ate. I can understand that,
as each Wednesday the menu was a total surprise to me as well.

Thien's typical meal starts with something light, such as seafood or a soup. This Vietnamese shrimp (*goi*) ceviche became an immediate hit on Fork's dinner menu after its first appearance at a Wednesday-night dinner.

vietnamese shrimp with fresh herbs (shrimp ceviche)

Serves 4 as an appetizer

12 to 16 shrimp with tails (16-to-20 size), deveined

water

1 Spanish onion, halved

8 garlic cloves

1 sprig fresh rosemary

1 sprig fresh thyme

2 to 3 sprigs fresh parsley

1 lemon, halved

salt

3 T olive oil

1 cup white wine

Place all ingredients except shrimp in a large pot. Bring to a boil. Add shrimp and boil 8 minutes. Remove from water to cool. Carefully peel shrimp, keeping tails intact.

½ cup extra-virgin olive oil

¼ cup lime juice

1 T fish sauce

½ red onion, half moon sliced

½ jalapeño, seeded and chopped

1 stalk celery, cleaned and sliced thin

1 T fresh mint leaves

1 T fresh cilantro, chopped

1 T fresh Thai basil leaves

2 T peanuts, crushed

When ready to assemble, mix olive oil, lime juice and fish sauce together. In a separate bowl, mix shrimp, onion, jalapeño and celery together. Coat with ¼ cup of olive oil mixture. Add additional liquid if necessary. Add herbs and toss gently. Serve on plates and sprinkle peanuts on top.

My family was always eating strange things like chicken feet, gizzards and tripe, so eating offal (the internal organs of an animal) has never bothered me. Thien was inspired to make this soup for Wednesday night after a trip to our favorite taqueria, La Lupe, in South Philadelphia, where we ate menudo. Menudo is a traditional, spicy Mexican soup made with tripe and other offal. Supposedly it is a cure for a hangover. You don't need a hangover to enjoy this dish, which is a tamer version of the Mexican one. You only have to eat tripe and baby octopus!

braised baby octopus and tripe with giant corn, guajillo chili sauce and tortillas

Serves 6 as a dinner main course

10 cups water

4 pounds plum tomatoes

4 jalapeño peppers

4 guajillo peppers or ancho chili peppers

8 cloves garlic

1 white onion

1 cup fresh cilantro

2 T ground cumin

2 T ground coriander

1 T oregano

juice of 2 limes

1 cup giant corn, canned or dried (prepared like dried beans; see sidebar on page 37)

1½ pounds honeycomb tripe

2 dozen baby octopus

twelve 9-inch flour tortillas, lightly grilled and placed in aluminum foil to stay warm

Bring 10 cups of water to a boil in a large stockpot, braiser or Dutch oven. Gently drop in tomatoes, jalapeño peppers, guajillo peppers, garlic and onion. Simmer about 5 minutes, until skins start to break. Drain into colander.

In batches, transfer tomatoes, peppers, garlic and onion to a food processor (or process in pot with an immersion blender). Add cilantro and lime juice. Process to a thick liquid. Add puréed tomatoes back into a pot. Add cumin, coriander and oregano, and stir to combine ingredients. Bring sauce to a boil and reduce heat to a simmer. Add tripe and giant corn. Simmer 2 to 3 minutes. Add octopus and simmer an additional few minutes. Ladle into warm bowls and serve with grilled tortillas.

When I learned that the *Philadelphia Inquirer's* food critic, Craig LaBan, had come to one of our Wednesday-night dinners at Fork:etc (see sidebar), I looked over the menu to recall what we had eaten that night. I know that Craig eats exotic foods, and I was pleased to see that Thien had made Tacos de Lingua (tongue tacos), which had been inspired by one of Thien's treks to La Lupe Taqueria in South Philadelphia.

tacos de lingua

Makes 12 to 16 tacos

TONGUE

1½ pounds beef tongue

1 Spanish onion

4 cloves garlic

1 bunch fresh cilantro

1 tsp ground cumin

1 tsp ground coriander

1 jalapeño pepper

salt and freshly ground black pepper to taste

Place all ingredients in a large stockpot. Turn heat to high until mixture is boiling. Reduce and simmer 3 hours, or until outer layer of tongue is falling off. Remove from heat and cool. Peel off outer layer. Slice thin.

PICO DE GALLO

4 plum tomatoes, seeded and diced into ¼- to ½-inch pieces

1 red onion, diced into ¼-inch pieces

1 jalapeño pepper, seeded and minced

2 radishes, diced into ¼-inch pieces

1 T extra-virgin olive oil

juice from two limes

2 T fresh cilantro, chopped fine

1 scallion, chopped fine

salt and freshly ground black pepper to taste

Combine ingredients together in a bowl. Mix gently.

grilled flour tortillas (wrap in aluminum foil to keep warm)

guacamole (see recipe on page 228)

pico de gallo

sour cream

Guajillo Chili Sauce (see recipe on page 234; substitute ½ cup of bittersweet dark chocolate chips for giant corn)

1 head romaine lettuce, cleaned and chopped

Prepare all ingredients. To assemble, place a few slices of tongue on each tortilla and roll tortilla into a cone. Serve on plate with chopped romaine and spoon 1 tablespoon each of guacamole, pico de gallo and sour cream on tacos. Serve ramekin of Guajillo Chili Sauce aside tacos.

People often ask me what it's like to be reviewed by a restaurant critic. It seems to me that I don't think about it that much, but if you ask my staff, they'll tell you that I'm obsessed. It's something that sneaks up on you, which is perhaps what I find unnerving. But all we can do is try to put out an honest product consistently at Fork--to provide food and service that are simple and unpretentious. Fork was reviewed by most food-oriented members of the Philadelphia press shortly after we opened, including the venerable Elaine Tait, the *Philadelphia Inquirer* food critic at that time. She retired shortly thereafter and Craig LaBan took over. Craig had a reputation from other cities as being tough. So of course I wanted him to approve of what we were doing at Fork. Craig's rating system involves bells: one bell is average, two is good, three is excellent and four is superior. My goal wasn't to get four bells, or even three. All I wanted was to know that he respected what we were doing.

The first time I suspected that he was at Fork was during the last few months of Anne-Marie's tenure; I was leaving for a long weekend and just happened to notice someone eating lunch and having a glass of wine at the bar. When I looked him straight in the eye, he looked down quickly and clearly felt uncomfortable. He started scribbling on a pad. I thought, "That's weird." And then I realized that he fit my image of the mysterious food critic. Immediately I warned the bartender that he might be Craig LaBan. Later, after Anne-Marie's departure, I felt that a review might be imminent, and I drove myself and everyone around me crazy. Every night I looked at every face, wondering if Craig LaBan was in the restaurant. (Unfortunately I couldn't remember what he looked like from that first sighting.) I went out two nights that winter— once to the orchestra and once to dinner. Both times, I entreated my veteran staff to keep up the vigilance. I warned them to be aware of anyone who orders more food than the number of guests at the table would need or anyone who asks more questions about the wine list than the average person might. But they didn't spot him. After his visit, as a part of the review process, he interviewed me and asked many questions about his meals. Following the interview, I went through all of our menus and bills to find the exact meals he had mentioned. Then I questioned the servers who had been assigned to his table on each dining occasion. And finally, I read his review. After all the anticipation, I was disappointed with our performance. I knew that our food overall was better than the meals he had experienced, but there was nothing I could do or say. All I could do was to work harder. When Craig published a book of his reviews, he updated the review, but even then I felt that it didn't reflect the amount of effort we put in.

The years passed, and I hadn't thought about Craig in a long time. Then one day Joanne Aretz, Bob's wife, asked me to come into Fork:etc to help her pick out some food for dinner. When I was at the counter, a voice that seemed very familiar asked the counter person a question about cheese. My Craig-dar was on! I knew he was standing in front of me. He confirmed this by asking a very specific question about an unusual cheese, a cheese that only a true foodie would know. I realized that he had just dined in the restaurant for lunch. So I went back into the restaurant and looked up his check to see what he had eaten. I still remember his meal, but if you were to ask me what he looks like, I couldn't tell you.

The clincher was that, a week later, he called me to arrange an interview, and when we spoke he started asking me about the previous week's chef's bistro dinner! I couldn't believe what I was hearing. The week before, I had eaten dinner with Craig LaBan in Fork:etc, elbow to elbow, and I hadn't even known it. I would have never guessed that he would show up at such a small venue. My boyfriend, Wayne, who has superhuman hearing and can listen to multiple conversations at the same time, told me that he had been able to tell that the man sitting next to him had eaten at a lot of places. Hats off to you, Craig. You got me!

coda

I've spent ten years in this dog-eat-dog world in which restaurants open and close regularly, new competition crops up every day and customer tastes are constantly changing. And throughout these years I have asked myself continually, "What makes Fork special?" Our original vision—to be an outstanding American bistro with good, unpretentious, tasty food—has continued to evolve. Cooking with fresh, seasonal ingredients has always been key, but that is not sufficient to set a restaurant apart from the myriads of others. Although restaurants follow trends in ingredients, the ethnic origins of dishes, plate sizes and styles of plating, when I think about what makes good, contemporary American food, I realize what wins me over: simplicity, honesty and interesting flavors.

But those dimensions alone won't make me remember a meal for years to come. Having eaten the majority of my meals over the past 3650 days outside of my home, I know what makes a meal truly memorable for me: a combination of great food and great company. I wonder if a part of what makes Fork special is the way our menu is created and inspired: during the great and unforgettable meals I have shared with friends and family, whether at home, at our Sunday-night and Wednesday-night meals, at a family meal at Fork or in another restaurant, whether locally or abroad.

Many of my friends tell me they think it must be great to own a restaurant and be able to dine there all the time, eating delicious food, drinking the best wines. True, it is wonderful when I actually get to sit back, look at the restaurant and enjoy these luxuries. But lately, the meal I crave more than anything is the most basic American meal: a great burger. It doesn't have to have fancy toppings. Good cheddar cheese, tomato and lettuce are enough.

People don't realize that making the perfect burger is not as simple as it seems. It must be cooked to the perfect temperature--so that it turns out medium rare--and be accompanied by crispy French fries. At Fork, we use ground sirloin and our housemade brioche bun. To make the fries crispy, we keep the oil hot and clean and double-fry the potatoes. A side of ketchup is a must. To me, nothing is more satisfying.

grilled hamburger with cheddar, tomato and lettuce aside crispy french fries

Serves 1

CRISPY FRENCH FRIES

2 Idaho potatoes, washed and cut
    into ½-inch fries

2 cups canola oil

salt and freshly ground black pepper
    to taste

Heat oil in a saucepot over medium heat. Cut potatoes and soak them in water to prevent discoloration. When the oil registers 370°F on a deep-fry thermometer, drain potatoes and pat them dry with a clean kitchen towel. Drop potatoes into oil and fry for 3 minutes. Remove from oil and drain in a wire basket or on a cookie sheet lined with a paper bag or paper towel. Let the oil temperature return to 370°. Just before serving burger, return potatoes to hot oil and fry an additional 3 minutes. Remove from oil, drain on paper towels and sprinkle with salt and pepper.

GRILLED HAMBURGER

8 ounces ground sirloin

salt and freshly ground black pepper

1 to 2 slices Vermont cheddar

1 ripe tomato, sliced

bibb lettuce leaves

1 brioche or roll of your choice

Preheat grill. Gently form a loose patty with the sirloin, about 1½ inches thick. Do not pack too tightly. Season with salt and pepper. When grill is very hot, place burger on grill and cook approximately 6 to 7 minutes on each side for medium rare. Cut brioche in half and toast lightly on grill while burger is cooking. Lay cheese on burger and cover for a minute. Remove burger and serve on bun with slices of tomato and bibb lettuce. Place fries on plate. Serve with ramekin of ketchup.

fork foundations

CHICKEN STOCK

Yields 4 quarts

6 quarts cold water

8 pounds chicken parts or whole chicken, cut up (including bones)

4 cups Spanish onions, chopped fine

2 cups carrots, chopped fine

2 cups celery, chopped fine

2 small heads of garlic

bouquet garni

To make bouquet garni for this recipe, wrap the following herbs and spices in a piece of cheesecloth: 1 teaspoon black peppercorns, 3 sprigs fresh parsley (including stems), 1 bay leaf, 1/2 bunch fresh thyme, 1/2 bunch fresh tarragon, 1/2 bunch fresh oregano and 1/2 bunch fresh sweet basil. Tie top closed with string.

To make stock, place chicken parts in a stockpot with water to cover and slowly bring to a simmer. Skim the top occasionally. Simmer 3 to 4 hours. Add onions, carrots, celery, garlic and bouquet garni. Simmer an additional hour. Do not stir. Set aside to cool, then strain stock through a chinois or a fine-mesh strainer.

If you will be using stock immediately, skim off fat. Otherwise you can wait until it has cooled, when fat will form a solid layer on top that is easy to remove. Do not refrigerate until stock is cool.

CLARIFIED BUTTER

Clarified butter, a pantry must, is butter that has had its whey and solids removed. Its use helps keep pan-fried or sautéed foods from becoming burned and spotted; it will also make your sautéed dishes look evenly cooked and clean. Clarified butter has a higher smoke point and more butter flavor than regular butter. It can be used to make traditional French brown butter, a bistro classic that is often served with skate or rainbow trout. Always use unsalted butter, as that way you can adjust the seasoning to taste. You can make a small or large batch, depending on preference, but use at least 1/2 pound of butter.

How to Clarify Butter

Place butter in a small saucepot and heat slowly over low to medium heat till it forms a layer of solids on top of a layer of clear fat. Remove from heat and let stand 20 minutes. Using a spoon, skim solids from top of butter. Then store. Clarified butter can be kept in the refrigerator for several months or frozen for up to 6 months.

DEMI-GLACE

A demi-glace is a rich brown sauce that forms the basis of many other sauces. If you decide to buy a demi-glace, D'Artagnan or Demi-Glace Gold are two reliable brands. To make your own, you can use either of two methods. One can be made in twenty-four hours by buying bones, roasting them and then cooking them with mirepoix, wine and tomato paste. The other method is the one we use in the restaurant. Because we have so many scraps, we make it several times a week with scraps of meat, chicken bones, vegetables and herbs. At home, you will need to collect these scraps and freeze them until you have saved enough.

Each of the recipes below yields about two gallons of stock, which you will reduce just before use. The bone method uses bones from the butcher that need to be roasted first, whereas the scrap method relies on you to collect food scraps in your kitchen.

BONE METHOD

10 pounds veal marrow bones and 8 pounds beef marrow bones (ask your butcher to cut them into 2- to 3-inch pieces)

Preheat oven to 450°F. Place bones in a roasting pan and roast for 1 hour, until bones are browned. Then follow instructions below Scrap Method.

SCRAP METHOD

For a month, save and freeze scraps of meat (fat removed as much as possible), meat bones and chicken bones until you have about 8 pounds. Then follow this recipe.

DEMI-GLACE

roasted bones or meat scraps

8 cups of mirepoix (4 cups Spanish
onions, chopped fine;
2 cups carrots, chopped fine;
2 cups celery, chopped fine)

1/2 cup fennel, coarsely chopped

1/2 cup parsnip, coarsely chopped

2 cloves garlic

1/2 cup olive oil or butter

one 16-ounce can tomato paste

2 sprigs fresh rosemary

2 sprigs fresh thyme

4 cups dry red wine

salt and black pepper

16 quarts of water

In a large Dutch oven or stockpot,
sauté mirepoix in olive oil over
medium heat for about 5 minutes.
Add fennel, parsnips and garlic and
continue sautéing mixture for an
additional 5 minutes. Deglaze pan
with 1/4 cup red wine. Add tomato
paste, salt and pepper. Place bones
in stockpot. Add remaining wine
and water. (If you have roasted
fresh bones, deglaze roasting pan
over medium heat with liquid from
stockpot, scraping bottom of pan
for brown particles. Add roasting
pan liquid to stockpot.) Bring liquid
to a boil, then reduce to a simmer.
Continue simmering for 6 hours.

Remove from heat. When liquid
has cooled, strain it through a chinois
or a tight-mesh strainer. Store in
containers in freezer and defrost
when needed. Before use, reduce
down to syrup over high heat.

MAYONNAISE

Here's a staple that's easy to make and
adds fresher flavor to recipes calling
for mayonnaise.

MAYONNAISE

1 egg yolk

1/4 tsp dry mustard

2 tsp lemon juice

salt and white pepper to taste

1 cup vegetable oil

1 T hot water

Whisk together egg yolk, mustard,
lemon juice, salt and pepper in
a large mixing bowl. Begin to add
about 1/4 cup vegetable oil, one drip
at a time. When mixture begins to
thicken, pour in remaining oil in a
very slow, steady stream, whisking
vigorously to emulsify mixture.
When a thick mayonnaise has formed,
gently whisk in hot water to set
the mixture. Use immediately or
put in tightly covered container
and refrigerate for a day or two.

MEAT STOCK

Meat stock is not a far departure
from demi-glace, so if you would
prefer something less rich, you can
reduce meat stock instead of creating
a demi-glace. In any case, meat stock
is a wonderful ingredient to use when
braising meat and making soups.

MEAT STOCK

Yields 4 quarts

6 quarts cold water

8 pounds meat trimmings
(of one type) with no fat

cooked or raw bones

4 cups Spanish onions, chopped fine

2 cups carrots, chopped fine

2 cups celery, chopped fine

2 small heads of garlic

bouquet garni containing 1 tsp black
peppercorn, 1 bunch fresh parsley,
1 bay leaf, 1 bunch fresh thyme,
1 bunch fresh tarragon, 1 bunch
fresh oregano and 1 one bunch
fresh basil

Place meat and bones in a stockpot
and cover with water. Slowly bring
liquid to a simmer. Skim off any scum
that forms. Simmer 3 to 4 hours. Add
mirepoix and bouquet garni. Simmer
for another hour. Do not stir. Set
aside to cool.

Strain stock through a chinois or
a fine-mesh strainer. If you are using
stock immediately, skim off fat;
otherwise, you can wait until it has
cooled and the fat has solidified.
Do not refrigerate until stock is cool.

illustration credits

The author and publisher gratefully acknowledge the following
for providing illustrations for this book.

BOB ARETZ page 12

WAYNE ARETZ pages 85, 162, 163

BRANCH CREEK FARM, pages 24, 103,
105, 187

PETE CHECCIA pages 3, 6, 8, 11, 13, 29, 40,
47, 48, 50, 51, 55, 60, 62, 66, 68, 80, 90, 92,
95, 110, 125, 135, 145, 152, 157, 160, 164,
172, 177, 178, 182, 194, 202, 203, 208, 224,
227, 231

ANTHONY DEMELAS page 57

SCOTT DONOHUE page 15

KAREN GIBSON page 56

KEVIN HILLS page 196

BOB KRIST page 4

WEAVER LILLEY page 5

PAUL RODRIGUEZ pages 58, 59

ROBERTO SELLA pages 170, 189, 195

DAVID SWANSON pages 30, 32, 100

ANNA TASCA LANZA page 181

TREVOR DIXON PHOTOGRAPHY pages 17,
43, 73, 74, 79, 82, 88, 96, 106, 113, 120,
127, 128, 136, 138, 139, 141, 149, 150, 158,
167, 168, 184, 190, 193, 212, 216, 219, 220,
223, 228, 233, 239, 240

MIH YIN page 2

ROY ZIPSTEIN pages 200, 215

The illustrations on pages 10, 34, 117,
118, 123 and 174 are from the author's
personal collection.

index

m